OTHER BOOKS by LOUIS SIMPSON

POETRY

The Arrivistes: Poems 1940–49
Good News of Death and Other Poems
A Dream of Governors
At the End of the Open Road
Selected Poems
Adventures of the Letter I

NONFICTION

James Hogg: A Critical Study
An Introduction to Poetry

FICTION

Riverside Drive

North
of
Jamaica

NORTH OF JAMAICA

Louis Simpson

HARPER & ROW, PUBLISHERS

NEW YORK, EVANSTON, SAN FRANCISCO, LONDON

Acknowledgment is made to the publishers who have granted permission to reprint poems in this book: "My Father in the Night Commanding No" and "Walt Whitman at Bear Mountain," copyright © 1963 by Louis Simpson, reprinted from *At the End of the Open Road*, by Louis Simpson, by permission of Wesleyan University Press; "My Father in the Night Commanding No" first published in *The New Yorker*. "Autumn Begins in Martin's Ferry, Ohio," copyright © 1962 by James Wright, reprinted from *The Branch Will Not Break*, by James Wright, by permission of Wesleyan University Press. "The Battle" reprinted by permission of Charles Scribner's Sons from *Good News of Death and Other Poems*, by Louis Simpson, copyright © 1955 by Louis Simpson *(Poets of Today II)*. "Squeal" reprinted by permission of *The Hudson Review*, copyright © 1957 by The Hudson Review, Inc. "Homage to Pablo Neruda, Perhaps" reprinted by permission of The Sixties Press; "Before the Poetry Reading" reprinted by permission of *The Listener*.

This book was published in England under the title *Air with Armed Men*.

This book is dedicated to my wife
Dorothy

I have no sympathy with the mid-Victorian thought to which Tennyson gave his support, that a poet's life concerns nobody but himself. A poet is by the very nature of things a man who lives with entire sincerity, or rather, the better his poetry the more sincere his life. His life is an experiment in living and those that come after have a right to know it. Above all, it is necessary that the lyric poet's life should be known, that we should understand that his poetry is no rootless flower but the speech of a man [that it is no little thing] to achieve anything in any art, to stand alone perhaps for many years, to go a path no other man has gone, to accept one's own thought when the thought of others has the authority of the world behind it . . . to give one's life as well as one's words which are so much nearer to one's soul to the criticism of the world.

W. B. YEATS

1

I

I watched Jabez cooking his midday meal. He placed a pan over some stones and piled twigs and sticks underneath. He was making dumplings.

Jabez was the garden-boy. His people came from Africa. My father said that they didn't like people to watch them eating. When my father came by, Jabez would cover his mouth with his hand. But he didn't mind if it was my brother or myself, and when he finished eating he would tell me a story.

One day Annancy and Brother Tiger went to the river to bathe.

"Annancy said to Tiger, 'Bro'er Tiger, so you are a big man, if you go in a river with your fat you a go drownded, so you fe take out your fat so lef' it here.' "

So Tiger left his fat on the river bank and went into the water. While he was bathing Annancy ate up Tiger's fat. After eating it he was afraid of Tiger and ran away.

He went to Little Monkey Town and he taught the monkeys to sing, "Yesterday this time me a nyam Tiger fat"—meaning, "Yesterday this time I ate Tiger's fat." The monkeys loved the song so much that they sang it over and over. Then they gave a ball, and there everyone was singing the song.

When Annancy got back to the river he found Tiger looking for his fat. Tiger said, "Bro'er Annancy, I can't find me fat at all." Then Annancy told him about the song the monkeys were singing. So Tiger and Annancy went to the

9

ball. They hid in the bush and heard the monkeys singing, "Yesterday this time me a nyam Tiger fat."

Then Tiger asked the monkeys for his fat. They said they didn't know anything about it—"Tis Mister Annancy larn us the song." Then Tiger wanted to fight the monkeys, but they sent to Big Monkey Town for some soldiers, and the soldiers came and flogged Brother Tiger and Annancy.

"So Bro'er Tiger have fe take bush an' Annancy run up a house-top."

From that time Tiger lives in the wood and Annancy in the house-top.

★

My father's people came from Scotland long ago. Aunt Annie sang:

> Maxwelton Braes are bonny
> Where early fa's the dew,
> And 'twas there that Annie Laurie
> Gie me her answer true.

She was an old lady in a black dress and high-buttoned shoes. She came driving up to the gate in a black buggy. Once she took a mango out of her handbag. The mango was soft and squashy. She told me to give it to the horse. I held out the mango and the horse turned his head quickly and snapped it out of my hand with his long yellow teeth. When he was eating the mango, yellow foam came down from his jaws.

My father's name was Aston Simpson and he was a lawyer. Every morning he went down town to the office.

One morning he said we were going to start doing exercises. It would help us to keep fit and grow strong. My father, my mother, my brother Herbert and I stood in front of the Victrola in our pyjamas. My father put a record on the Victrola, "*The Stars and Stripes Forever*—march—Sousa". Above the band a man's voice shouted in time to the music, "Feet apart! Hands on hips, place! Now, bend forward—up! To the left—up! To the right—up!"

Then we got dressed and had breakfast. Father was dressed in a white suit. When he went to work he wore a Panama hat and carried a leather bag. He drove a red Essex. I could hear the engine starting, then going down the driveway. It turned into the lane and then I could no longer hear it.

After breakfast my mother sat at the piano, practising. She made a humming sound in her throat and sang, "Do-re-me-fa-so-la-di!" She sang songs from *Samson* and *Lucia di Lammermoor*. Her voice was loud, and there was something about it that frightened me. When she sang she had a far-away look on her face. I pressed my hands to my ears.

Once she saw me doing this, and asked if I didn't like her singing. I didn't know what to say. She went away with a hurt look on her face.

But I liked the Victrola. She would put on a record and I would wind it up. The handle was hard to turn. "Gems from Pagliacci"—it began with bells and voices. "Floradora." I could hardly make out the words; they came with a faint scratching from a great distance, across the sea.

I looked at the pictures in the *Victor Book of the Opera*. There were photographs of fat men and women with odd names—Galli-Curci, Melba, Scotti, Schumann-Heinck, Caruso. They wore jewellery and tights. They brandished swords, rode in boats pulled by swans, leaned out from balconies. One man was lying flat on his back, with lighted candles at his head and feet. On another page I came upon the same scene, but with a different man lying on his back. How could this be? Wasn't the story true?

In the twilight, when fireflies were glimmering, my father came home from the office. I could hear his car turning on the gravel into the driveway. Sometimes when he came up the stairs on to the veranda he would be carrying a rolled-up newspaper. This was the *Daily Mirror*, all the way from England. There were funny-cuts in it, about a dog named Pip, a penguin named Squeak, and a rabbit named Wilfred. There were also a Russian dog named Popsky and his master, Witoffsky. Popsky and Witoffsky made bombs. When the policeman came in his helmet they ran away.

Once when my father came home he was carrying a round leather case. He opened it and took out a tube of brass. He said it was a telescope. He pulled at one end of the tube and it got longer. There was a circle of glass at each end. He placed the telescope on a stand on the veranda, and when it got dark we took turns looking through the eyepiece.

I looked at the moon; it was bright as a shilling. There were shadows on the face of the moon. A sea breeze rustled the vines that grew on the veranda, and a lizard hopped on to the railing. It cocked its head sideways, looking at us, and puffed out the wattle under its throat in a threatening manner. There were millions of glittering stars. He said that if I looked I would see the constellations.

At bedtime Mother would read us stories. She read a story called *The Happy Prince*. Or else she would tell stories about Russia when she was a child. Russia was covered with snow and the wind was freezing cold. Wolves howled in the distance. People rode in sleighs with jingling bells. In Russia there were cossacks. . . .

"What are cossacks?"

"People who ride horses. There were also gypsies and moujiks."

"What's a moujik."

"A Russian. One of the people."

It was so cold in Russia that people froze to death and were found the next day with ice on their faces. Once on her way to school she was almost frozen. Her hands and feet were numb, and she was shivering all day.

Also, in Russia there was a terrible sickness called typhus.

She was sick with typhus and almost died. But for a woman who lived next door and took care of her, she would have died. Her older sister Lisa was sick too, and her mother was taking care of Lisa. So nobody paid her any attention, except the woman who lived next door. When she was well again they brought her a mirror, and when she looked into it she hardly knew herself. They had cut off her hair. And they had burned all her clothes, and burned her doll—she had never had a real doll of her own, only a stick which she dressed in rags, and they had burned it. Then they told her that her sister Lisa had died.

They sent her away to Odessa on the Black Sea, for her health, to stay with relatives. Odessa was a big town—not like Lutsk, where her family lived. On the last day in Odessa she wanted to buy a present to take back to the family. She had saved all her money. She saw a basket of plums in a window.

"What are plums?"

"Fruit."

"Like bananas?"

She laughed. "Oh no. Much better than bananas. Small and round, with red inside. Sweet and delicious."

She bought the plums. No one in Lutsk had ever been able to buy them. They would be pleased.

But the train took days to go from Odessa to Lutsk. The weather was warm and the plums started to spoil. She didn't know what to do. What would you have done?

I'd heard the story before, so I said, "Eat them."

"Yes, I ate them, so they wouldn't be wasted. When one of the plums got soft, I ate it. So I ate them one by one, and soon the basket was half empty. And every time I ate one of the plums I would cry, because I didn't want to eat them, you know, I wanted to give them to my mother and my sisters. The people on the train were astonished—a child who would eat a plum and cry!"

13

When she got off the train at Lutsk the basket was empty.

When she had kissed me good-night and tucked me in, I lay awake, with the moon shining through the window. The same moon shone in Russia, on the plains covered with snow and the people dressed in furs, riding in sleighs, with jingling bells. In the distance a wolf was howling. It was the same moon shining here. The moon came all the way from Russia, to shine here in the tropics, on the sea and the mountains.

II

Mummy would be proud of me when she came back. Did I know where Mummy was? Yes, that was right, in America.

America was a place with tall buildings called skyscrapers. Did I know what Americans did that was important to us?

Yes, they made movies. But also they ate sugar and bananas. Jamaica sent lots of bananas in ships to New York and the people who lived there bought them and ate them. And with the money they paid for bananas and oranges and grapefruit we were able to buy the things we needed—such as motor-cars and iceboxes. For everything had a purpose.

The cat came into the room, with a lizard in its mouth. It was a green tree lizard; its mouth was gaping.

"Shoo!" Miss Haughton shouted. She stamped her foot and the cat ran across the room, purposefully, carrying the lizard. It went out the door.

Once Mummy saw a cat with a mouse and she screamed.

There were bubbles at the corners of her mouth. And once when I was talking to her, facing her, I saw a mouse run along the wall. She saw where I was looking, and she didn't turn her head, but she became still and said, "What is it? What is it?" Then the mouse vanished, and I was too frightened to tell her. So I said nothing.

In Lutsk when she was a child there were swarms of rats. They carried the typhus that made people die. And they crawled over the faces of people in the night. Rats lived in the attics of houses.

What's an attic?

The dark part of the house between the ceiling and the roof. The rats lived there, and if a child went in they would swarm over him, biting off his fingers. They would eat him all up.

I was frightened of the rats. She talked about them often, how they would bite children and eat them.

It was to get away from the rats that she and her family went to America. They lived in New York, and she went to work. She was only a young girl, but she had to work hard, in a loft with a lot of other young girls.

What's a loft? Like an attic?

No, she laughed. It seemed to please her that I remembered about the attic and the rats. In the loft the girls sat working at sewing-machines, making dresses and pieces of clothing. It was hot and crowded. Her arms ached from guiding the pieces of cloth into the machine, and at the end of the day she was glad to get home, walking through the streets of New York. In the winter going home it was dark, and snowflakes came whirling down between the lights, the lights of New York City.

She lived with her mother and two sisters, Ruth and Annette, and a brother named Joe, and two nieces named Molly and Dorothy whom her mother also took care of. Molly's and Dorothy's mother had been Lisa.

15

The one who died in the typhus epidemic?

That's right. And her mother, my grandmother, was taking care of them all. But Mummy had to work in the loft, with the sewing-machines, all day long.

And then one day a man came.

Oh yes, tell about it!

A man came into the loft, and the foreman—the man who walked up and down the rows of machines, watching so that the girls didn't stop working—told them that the strange man was going to speak to them, and to stop the machines. Then the strange man said that he was from a motion-picture company, and they were looking for girls to try out for parts. So the next day she went to the address that he gave.

What did it look like?

It was a swimming-pool, that was where they were making the screen-tests. The test was to jump into the pool and pretend to be drowning. And I went up to the side of the pool and looked down. I couldn't swim at all.

Then I jumped.

I was really drowning, but they thought I was a wonderful actress. And so I was hired and became one of the motion-picture company, one of Annette Kellerman's Bathing Beauties. Then one day the company travelled to Jamaica to make a movie, and I met your father. And so we were married.

And lived happily ever after.

On Saturdays Nanny took me to the movie matinee at Cross Roads. This was at the Movie Theatre, which was indoors. I saw Rin-Tin-Tin, and Laurel and Hardy, and Louise Fazenda. On Saturday nights my father would take us to the Gaiety Theatre. It was open and you could see the sky. But we stopped going there because the English soldiers and the black people got into fights. The soldiers fought with their belt buckles.

16

The Palace was the best of all. It was an open-air theatre like the Gaiety. We sat upstairs in the balcony. First there were advertisements for Issa's Store, and Delaware Punch, and Four Aces. There would be a cartoon, Felix the Cat, or Mickey Mouse. And then—

> *Rio Rita*
> *The Cat and the Canary*
> *Evergreen*—with Jessie Matthews

> > It's the loveliest theeng
> > To be evergreen,
> > It's the loveliest theeng, I know . . .

"But you're not doing your letters!" said Miss Haughton. "You've only copied three letters in all this time."

The letters of the alphabet marched down the left side of the page. I was supposed to dip the point of the pen in the ink and copy each letter ten times, all the way across the page.

"Don't you want to learn, so that you'll know how to write when Mummy comes back?"

★

"If your Mother loved you," said Aunt Ethel, "she'd be here with her children. Not in New York City."

My bottom lip trembled. A weight seemed to be dragging down the corners, and my eyes were filling with tears. I turned my head aside. I wasn't going to let her see me cry. But it didn't help . . .

"What are you crying about?" said Aunt Ethel. She enjoyed these heart-to-heart talks.

Aunt Ethel was my father's sister, and had come to stay and take care of us while Mummy was away in America. She wore glasses and smelled of eau-de-cologne. On Sundays she took us to church.

Onward Christian so-o-o-old-iers
Marching as to-o war,
With the cross of Je-sus,
Go-ing on before!

Aunt Ethel saw that I washed behind my ears. "Let's look at the potato patch," she'd say. She saw to it that my nails were clean and that there were no spots on the suit I put on in the afternoon when we had tea.

My brother Herbert said that Aunt Ethel was an "old maid".

"What's that?"

"Nobody ever wanted to marry her."

Herbert played a trick on Aunt Ethel. He put a dead frog in her bed, and that night when father came home he called for me. I went into the study. My father was sitting down and Herbert was standing in front of him.

My father said to me, "Did you put a frog in your aunt's bed?"

I was so frightened I hardly knew what to answer. But I shook my head. No.

"Liar!" my father shouted at Herbert. Then, to the air over his head, "The boy is not only mischievous, he's also a liar."

To Herbert, "Well, I'll see to it that you don't play any more dirty tricks. And tell the truth."

He left the study and shouted for the servants. They came in, the maid, then the cook, wiping her hands on her apron. Their eyes were wide and they looked frightened. Aunt Ethel didn't come—she was in her bedroom, crying because she had been insulted.

When my father came back into the room he was carrying the leather strap on which he sharpened his razor.

"Take down your trousers," he said to Herbert.

Herbert took down his trousers. I could see his bottom.

Then my father seized him and in a moment he was sitting down, with Herbert lying face down across his lap. He lifted the strap and brought it down. There was a crack, and a red welt across Herbert's bottom. He shouted "No!" and kicked out his legs.

My father brought down the strap again and again. Herbert yelled and wept.

Cook said, "Lawks, Massa Aston, that sufficient!" But my father continued to flog Herbert.

At last he let him go. Herbert ran out of the room.

"Let that be a lesson to you too," my father said. "Not to tell lies."

When I went into the nursery Herbert was hiding under the bed. He came out and grabbed me by the arm. He was eleven years old, five years older than I, and much stronger.

He bent my arm behind my back. I uttered a cry.

"What's this?" said my father. He appeared in the doorway. "Are you bullying your brother? Do you want me to give you another flogging?"

He went away. Herbert glared at me. Then he put his hands to his cheeks and pulled them down. The flesh was drawn away from the bones and I could see the outlines of a skull. The Phantom of the Opera.

III

"Why don't you say anything," Mother said, "aren't you glad to see me?" She smelled of perfume. She hugged us to her and tears ran down her face. She was laughing and crying at the same time.

She let us watch while she unpacked her trunks. She had beautiful dresses and jewellery. Then she took out a box wrapped in paper. And another. They were presents for us. Mine was a train that you wound up and it ran on a track.

And books. *Black Beauty. Penrod and Sam. Tarzan and the Jewels of Opar.*

That night at the dinner table everyone was talking, and my father didn't seem to mind. Aunt Ethel smiled and made a remark now and then too, but I could tell she wasn't really pleased. Now she would have to go away. She wouldn't be keeping an eye on us and she wouldn't be taking us to church on Sunday.

"Good riddance," Herbert said.

The house had been getting quieter and quieter, especially in the evening when my father was home. But now it was noisy again. Mother played the piano and sang:

> Pale hands I loved
> Beside the Shalimar . . .

"We ought to give a party," she said.

My father said, "For what reason? I can't just ask people to come to a party."

"Why not? I'll tell them it's my birthday."

He laughed. He didn't seem to mind if she told a lie.

Everyone talked about the party for days. It was to be a "lawn tennis party". The garden-boy was put to work, rolling the tennis court and clipping hedges. The maid polished the silver, and some new records for the gramophone came from a store on King Street. Mother wouldn't let us play them, we could only look at the names. "Valencia", "Nola". We couldn't play them because they were for dancing, and we might scratch or break them.

"There ought to be something for the children too," Mother said. "They could have a fancy-dress party. And play games, like Pin the Tail on the Donkey."

Herbert and I were to be pirates. We would have red bandanas around our heads and scarfs round our waists, and we would each have a sword. Mother painted a moustache on my face, with pointed ends. Like Henry Morgan the Buccaneer. Yo ho ho and a bottle of rum.

"Well, that does it," my father said. "The Manleys aren't coming."

"Why? What does he say?"

"That Mrs. Manley isn't feeling well. But that's not true. The fact is, he knows he isn't welcome in this house."

Mother said, "They came to dinner."

"Yes, with other coloured people—to use your very own words. And Norman Manley is the most brilliant barrister on the island. A Rhodes Scholar."

Mother was silent.

"I'm coloured myself," he said, "or haven't you heard about it?"

Still she didn't say anything.

He said, "I can't arrange my life according to your likes and dislikes. The people I work with are a damn sight better than the people from the Liguanea Club you think are so wonderful. I have to work with Norman Manley. Moreover, his wife is a white woman. She's English. That ought to please you." His voice took on the sarcasm my brother and I knew so well, and he imitated our mother's way of speaking: "I love the way the English pronounce their words."

That night in the bedroom Herbert and I discussed this conversation.

"You're coloured," Herbert said.

"I'm not." I didn't know what "coloured" meant, but I didn't like the way he said it. I held up my hand in the moonlight. It looked yellow.

"You are," said Herbert.

"Well, then," I said, with a feeling of triumph I hardly ever had in these arguments, "you're coloured too."

Herbert jumped out of bed. I heard him coming, and pushed as hard as I could against the wall. But he hit me on the arm.

"That'll teach you to be rude and impertinent."

On the day of the party the lane was filled with cars. All kinds of people came—my mother's friends from the Liguanea Club and my father's friends, solicitors, barristers, and clerks. The men wore blazers and white flannels, and the women wore white skirts. They were carrying tennis rackets. On the lawn they leaped about, striking at the balls, and the garden-boy, who served for every purpose and had been dressed in white for the occasion, ran up and down in the hedge looking for lost balls.

Behind the base-line, card tables had been set up with glass pitchers of ice and lemonade and decanters of whisky that glowed amber in the sunlight. There were open tins of Players cigarettes; on the label there was a picture of a bearded sailor and a "dreadnought". The people who were not playing sat in deck chairs and now and then one of them would call out, "Well played!" My father leaped about with the rest. He came off the court wiping sweat from his brow.

"Jolly well played, Aston," said one of the young men. He was a clerk in my father's office. He was fat and brown, and spoke with a Jamaican accent. I had seen him when I was taken to the office, coming in to stand in front of my father's desk, holding a paper in his hand. "Well, give it here," said my father, irritably. "You'd damn well better have it right this time." But now he was calling my father "Aston", and my father smiled and didn't seem to mind.

The children were having their fancy-dress party. We played Pin the Tail on the Donkey. It was my turn and I was blindfolded. I went toward the tree where the donkey had been pinned, but I couldn't find it.

"Never mind," Mother said. "You can have a prize too."

This gave me a funny feeling. I had tried very hard to

22

stick on the tail, and if I was going to get a prize anyway, it seemed that my trying so hard didn't count.

Then there were prizes for costumes. Mother gave the first prize to Herbert and myself for our pirate costumes. The other children looked sulky. Then she gave them prizes too. So all the children were happy.

When it grew dark and the swallows dipping over the court began to be mistaken for tennis balls, everyone went inside. Mother put a record on the Victrola, and the young people danced.

> Valencia,
> In my dreams it always seems
> I hear you calling me . . .

The fat brown clerk from my father's office stood at the side of the drawing-room smiling at everyone. I was standing beside him, watching the dancers.

"Oh, jolly well danced," he said loudly. My father came by. "This isn't the tennis court, Henriques," he said. The clerk was silent and I felt sorry for him.

Then everyone went home. I stood in the lane watching them driving away. The English people from the Liguanea Club got into their Baby Austins and waved good-bye. The clerk had a motor-cycle, which he started with a roar. Then they were all gone.

The next day the lawn was littered with cigarette butts, tinfoil and empty packets. There were glasses under the hedge. The garden-boy was cleaning the lawn. He picked up all the cigarette butts and put them in a can. He smoked them for weeks, taking a butt out of the can after he had eaten lunch.

"Players are best," he said, with the air of a connoisseur. "But Four Aces are also very good."

From time to time as he went about his duties in the yard he would stop and make striking motions with an imaginary

23

tennis racket. Then he'd say, "Jolly well played." And sometimes, "Oh, hard luck!"

Then he'd shake his head, and go back to pushing the lawn-mower.

IV

Arithmetic: Eight times eight are sixty-four.

History: Jamaica was first inhabited by Arawak Indians. The name Jamaica comes from an Arawak word meaning "isle of wood and water".

The island was discovered by Columbus (1494) and colonized by the Spaniards, who introduced slavery. In 1655 Jamaica was captured by the British. Today, with its crops of sugar-cane, citrus fruits, and bananas, the island is one of the brightest jewels in the crown of Empire.

Eight times nine are seventy-two.

After lunch we played in the school yard. There was a tamarind tree. Pods fell from the boughs and lay scattered on the ground. If you opened them there were seeds inside covered with sticky brown stuff—sweet, but it set your teeth on edge.

After school the chauffeur came to pick me up and take me home. But one day, instead of the chauffeur, it was Aunt Ethel.

She said, "You're to stay with Uncle Percy and Aunt Agnes."

"Can't I go home?"

"Not tonight. Maybe tomorrow."

We travelled in a tram-car to the South Camp Road. When we got there Aunt Agnes showed me to a room where my cousin Nigel slept. She said I would share the bed with Nigel.

"But I want to go home."

"You have to stay with us for a while. Your Mummy and Daddy are very busy and they said you are to stay with us."

There were Aunt Agnes and Aunt Ethel, and cousins Gwen and Dora. They sat on the veranda fanning themselves.

"Where is the boy?" said Aunt Ethel.

"I left him in the bedroom to rest," said Aunt Agnes.

But I wasn't in the bedroom, I was on the other side of the door.

"I knew no good would come of that marriage."

"What is to become of the children?"

Later my cousin Nigel came home—he whose bed I was to share. Nigel was older than my brother Herbert. He went to Jamaica College, where he was good at games. He was also a brilliant student. "Come on," he said, "I'll teach you how to play marbles." He had a can full of glass marbles, shining, with whorls of colour. Some of the marbles were white and twice as big as the others. He took me out to the yard and drew a circle in the dust. He put twelve marbles in the circle. Eight twelves are ninety-six. He held a marble between his thumb and forefinger, then flicked his thumb. The marble shot against the marbles in the circle and four rolled out. Four from twelve leaves eight.

I tried, but I couldn't do it. My marble missed the circle entirely. I burst into tears.

"You shouldn't cry over a game," Nigel said. "Only girls cry." Then he said, "Come on then, let's do something else."

"I don't want to do anything. I want to go home."

"Would you like to see the turkeys?"

I nodded, and he led me round the house to the back yard.

There were turkeys, ducks and chickens walking up and down.

"Here," he said, "here's a turkey feather. See, if you let it go it flies like an aeroplane."

It was true. The feather drifted slowly to the ground. Each of us held a feather and let it go. They collided and whirled down, falling more quickly.

"Look at this," he said. He was holding out a winged seed. "Doesn't it look like an aeroplane propeller?"

It was true. It did.

I walked toward my Camel. I climbed into the cockpit, and the mechanic stood by the propeller.

"Contact!"

The engine burst into life with a roar. There was a smell of castor oil. The plane trembled, pressing against the chocks. The rest of the squadron was warming up. I pulled the goggles down over my eyes, raised my gloved hand and let it fall. My plane rolled forward, bumping, gathered speed, and the ground fell away beneath.

The squadron flew east, into the clouds streaked with rays of the rising sun. The dawn patrol. We passed over a village and the people waved. We were flying over trenches and barbed wire; then No Man's Land. I could see the shell holes. The poor bloody infantry!

Below me, close to the ground, I saw a Hun two-seater sneaking back to the German lines. A sitting duck—but I had more important business in hand.

Young Charteris was lagging. I throttled back and flew alongside his plane, motioning with my hand—"Keep up!" Why did they send us these youngsters? Yesterday we'd lost two. They had probably had only twenty hours' flying time between them.

I fired a burst to clear the guns . . .

"Coo-e-e-e!" That was Aunt Ethel calling from the house. Nigel went ahead and I followed.

We sat at a long table. Everyone became silent, and Uncle Percy, sitting at the head of the table, closed his eyes and said, "For these and all his mercies may the Lord's name be praised." Uncle Percy worked at the Institute of Agriculture. Nigel's older brother Dennis was also present. He was articled to my father and worked in his law office. Everyone was busy eating. The food was different from the kind we had at home. There were big dishes filled with sticky white rice, and pieces of boiled breadfruit, and a dish full of yellow yam, mashed up. It all tasted alike. There were no green vegetables. The meat was odd-looking—flat and white with holes in it.

"What is it?" I asked.

"That's tripe," said Aunt Agnes. The meat had a strong smell like when you went to the toilet. I pushed my plate away.

"Don't be rude," said Aunt Ethel.

"Waste not, want not," said Cousin Dora, who was sitting on the other side of the table. Then she giggled. She was fat and silly.

Cousin Gwen, who was sitting next to me, pushed my plate back in place, and whispered, "Be a good boy. Show them how well you can behave."

I picked up my fork and tasted the tripe again. It wasn't so bad, if you didn't think about going to the toilet. I ate a spoonful of rice. I was hungry.

After dinner I followed Dennis. He went into a bedroom and stood in front of a mirror brushing his hair and humming.

I said, "What happened to my father?"

He was startled. "What do you mean what happened?"

"They won't let me go home, and they talk about my mother and father."

I was once more on the verge of tears.

Dennis hummed. It was a tune of the year called "La

27

Cucaracha". I had heard that he liked to go dancing at the Silver Slipper. Aunt Ethel said that Dennis thought he was a "lady's man", and my father said that he was the "black sheep of the family".

He finished brushing his hair and looked at himself in the mirror. He met my eye and winked. Then he whistled a tune called "Green Eyes".

"The ladies," he said, "the ladies."

I bit my lip to keep back the tears. How could he be so stupid! Why wouldn't he tell me?

He put a straw hat on his head and tilted it at a becoming angle. He took a pack of cigarettes from the bureau and put it in his side pocket. He raised his left foot and polished the toe of his shoe with his handkerchief. Then his right shoe. He put the handkerchief back in his breast pocket.

"Ask me no questions," he said, "and I'll tell you no lies."

He winked again and went away, humming "La Cucaracha".

*

My brother Herbert was now at a boarding-school in Mandeville so I had no one to confide in. Nigel was always busy, kicking a football, hitting a tennis-ball against the door of the garage. By the thumping of the tennis-ball you could tell when he was home. Also he collected postage stamps and tram tickets—green tickets in one packet, white in another. He had a shoe-box full of tickets, each packet neatly tied with a rubber band.

In the evenings Nigel had to do lots of homework. I watched as he covered pages with adding, subtracting, multiplying, dividing. And this was only a beginning. He worked with a compass and a ruler, making circles and triangles and rectangles with letters of the alphabet at the corners and numbers along the sides. He was also learning algebra.

$5ab \times 3a^2b^3 = 15a^3b^4$. When I was as old as Nigel, even the letters of the alphabet would have turned into sums.

He was learning Latin. There were parallel columns of Latin nouns and verbs to be learned by heart, and no sooner had he memorized one set of columns than he had to memorize another. Also he had to study English, which consisted of learning poems by heart. He handed me the book and told me to follow the lines on the page and to stop him if he made a mistake. He closed his eyes and said very quickly:

> Lars Porsena of Clusium
>> By the Nine Gods he swore
> That the great house of Tarquin
>> Should suffer wrong no more.
> By the Nine Gods he swore it,
>> And named a trysting day,
> And bade his messengers ride forth,
> East and west and south and north,
>> To summon his array.

In this way he had learned hundreds of lines which he could recite without stopping and without making a mistake. He was the best at English in his class.

This would prove useful later on, for Nigel was going to be a lawyer, like my father. His older brother Dennis was already articled, but it was Nigel who had the brains and worked hard, while Dennis stayed out late at night. One night Dennis didn't come home until very late, and when he did he was wearing a paper hat and blowing a paper trumpet. He said "Yippee!" three times, then he went to bed. The next morning, which was Sunday, everyone spoke in hushed tones; Aunt Ethel said that Dennis was going to bring his father to an early grave.

On Saturday mornings we went swimming. Aunt Agnes, Aunt Ethel and Cousin Dora didn't like the water, but

Uncle Percy, Nigel and I, and cousin Gwen—who was a sport though she was a girl—set off in the car. It was an old Ford and it rattled. We drove through Kingston and then the streets began to thin out. We were getting close to the beach. We saw coconut trees and huts roofed with sheets of zinc and palm leaves. Then the bathhouse and the sea breaking in long lines of white surf.

We swam in an enclosure. Wooden posts painted with tar had been driven into the floor of the harbour, making four sides, and wire mesh was attached to the posts. This was to keep out sharks and barracudas. The wind was strong, and waves came rolling in to break on the sand. We frolicked in the waves, splashing each other. We dived down to the bottom. It was dark and muddy on the bottom. There was seaweed and also sea-eggs with prickles. If you got a prickle in your foot it would have to be taken out with a needle.

The coconut trees tossed in the wind and the coconuts thudded together. Across the harbour we could make out the blue line of the Palisadoes, stretching toward Port Royal. Gulls were beating against the wind. Now and then one would swoop down and make a splash and rise with a fish in its beak. On some rotting posts close to the shore perched a group of pelicans, each solitary on its post, its beak tucked in its chest. From time to time one of the pelicans would extend bat-like wings and fly creakily away.

When we came back from swimming we were tired and happy.

Sunday was a day of rest. Uncle Percy, Aunt Agnes, Aunt Ethel and my cousins Gwen and Dora sat in rocking-chairs on the veranda, fanning themselves and looking across the South Camp Road at the hills in the distance. You could hear the tramline starting to hum. Then you heard the tram coming a long way off. It made a grinding sound on the rails. Then it stopped. The bell clanged and the tram started again. The sound got louder. The tram went by; you could

30

see people sitting on the benches with a railing along the side. The better-dressed people were on the front benches. Then the sound of the tram grew fainter and died away.

A john crow flew over, very high, gliding in lazy circles.

On Sunday I had to sit still. I wasn't allowed to play games like tiddly-winks and snakes-and-ladders or run around in the yard. I could read a book if it wasn't too exciting.

At the midday meal on Sunday, grace was twice as long as usual. We ate for a long time, and after lunch everyone went off to take a nap. I had to lie down and not make any noise. I had some halves of walnut shells under my pillow. I pushed them along the sheet. *England expects every man to do his duty.* I had a handful of small brass cartridges Nigel had given me. He was on the rifle team at school. *Up Guards and at 'em!*

In the afternoon again we sat on the veranda, and in the evening we went to church. I stood beside Cousin Gwen, looking into the black hymn-book.

> How sweet the name of Je-sus sounds
> In a believer's ear.

On the way home from church my aunts and cousins discussed the service and the minister's sermon. Aunt Ethel had almost married a minister, Reverend Jones. When his name was mentioned she pursed her mouth and shook her head. She had refused to marry Reverend Jones in order to help her sister Agnes to raise her family. It was a sacrifice. We must sacrifice our own selfish desires so that we may do the will of our Lord.

V

Then I was home with my father again, and Herbert was home from boarding-school. I watched him unpacking his trunk. Everything smelled mouldy and his khaki school clothes were stained with "red dirt". His school, he said, was on a mountain that was all composed of that bleeding substance. He showed me a slingshot, and a wooden gig with a sharp metal point, and a piece of flint.

As soon as Aunt Ethel—once more in charge of the household and supervising this unpacking—was out of earshot, I asked where Mother was. Had she gone to America again?

"She's right here in Kingston," Herbert said in a whisper, "staying at the Manor House Hotel, at Constant Springs."

"How do you know?"

"She wrote me a letter at school."

But why wasn't she living with us? Herbert did not know the answer. Nor was Aunt Ethel any more enlightening. She said, "Oh, go away. Don't bother me! There are things you children shouldn't know."

With a certain delicacy I sensed that as my father had not told us, he must not want to. There were reticences, dumb depths, that must not be stirred. It would be shameful on my part to ask him where my mother was. Every morning he went to work as usual, and the household went about its business, the housemaid on her knees smearing the floor with beeswax and thumping it with a brush of coconut fibre. She washed down the veranda with a mop. I stared into the bucket in which "civil" orange halves were floating. It was as though my mother had never existed. I went into

her bedroom and looked in a closet. There were still a few
dresses on hangers, smelling of perfume, hat-boxes and beads
on the floor.

I tried reading *The Happy Prince*, the story she had liked
reading aloud at bedtime. And the books she brought from
America. There was a set of books called *Journeys Through
Bookland*. Book I was for the nursery, Book II for children
learning to read, and so on, increasing in difficulty. The
books were illustrated with drawings in line and colour.
I opened one of the middle volumes and came upon a
picture that made me jump—of a skeleton sitting bolt
upright, a thing of bones and ribs, wearing a suit of armour.
The eyes of the skull were hollow, the jaws were open, and
one fleshless hand was raised in the air.

> Speak! speak! thou fearful guest!
> Who, with thy hollow breast
> Still in rude armour drest,
>   Comest to daunt me!
> Wrapt not in Eastern balms,
> But with thy fleshless palms
> Stretched, as if asking alms,
>   Why dost thou haunt me?

This must be poetry, for the lines on the page were short,
each began with a capital letter, the ends of lines sounded
alike, and the words were not the words that people used,
so that I could hardly tell what they meant.

Then, starting from the page, a line that mystified me . . .
Speaking of the "maiden" in the story, the skeleton said,
"She was a mother." Hadn't she always been a mother?
Could it happen suddenly? If she hadn't always been a
mother, what had she been?

The next line said: "Death closed her mild blue eyes."
She was a mother and then she died.

I read through to the end. The Viking fell on his spear

and his soul, "Bursting these prison bars", fled into the sky. The story ended with a frightening shout: "*Skoal!* to the Northland! *Skoal!*"

The volume exerted a dreadful fascination. Whenever I was in my father's study, where the books were kept, I knew that this book was there, with the picture of the skeleton, the maiden of whom it was said that "Death closed her mild blue eyes", and the word "*Skoal!*" that sounded like "skull".

★

Our father was not a religious man, and though he let Aunt Ethel take us to church, he himself spent his Sundays in the "carpenter's shop" where he hammered, sawed and filed. He liked using his hands, filing pieces of brass and iron to one purpose and another. A leaky faucet could keep him happy for hours. If only life could be banged and twisted so that it ran properly!

My toy train kept flying off the track. He stuck a wad of putty on to the engine. This slowed it down so that it did not fly off the track. I could no longer imagine that the thing with a lump of putty on its side was a locomotive engine, but he looked on with a satisfied expression. He didn't care what things looked like as long as they worked.

On this principle he set about making a model steam boat. Finally it was five feet long, standing on the trestle. It had a round boiler in the middle from which a steam gauge protruded. Steam jetted out, the propeller whirled, and the trestle shook. He took this machine down to the Yacht Club on a Sunday and sent it plowing through the waves in a circle. It was watertight, unsinkable, and unconvincing. In contrast, there was a model frigate belonging to one of the members—it had billowing sails and little guns that slid in and out; when it passed over the waves you could imagine the seamen on board and hear the boatswain's whistle. You could almost see Horatio Nelson on the quarter-deck.

He put the steam-boat on the trestle again, in order to carry out some further improvements.

I said, "Why don't you get a real boat?"

He stopped work, chisel in hand, and looked at me seriously. I had never before said anything that made such an impression. Within the month he had bought a real boat—a motor-boat with an outboard engine, and it lay bobbing offshore at the Yacht Club. But though the boat was real, it managed nevertheless not to look like a boat. Whereas all the other boats anchored offshore had a bow, my father's boat had a blunt end, as though it had been cut short for the sake of economy.

He entered it in a few races. But though he was willing to race, he was somewhat cautious, or else the shape of the boat was wrong, for he always came in last. I grew embarrassed watching him.

In one race the contestants were to come in to shore, pick up a passenger, and go out again. He told me to stand on the dock and to jump into the boat when he gave the signal. I watched the boats cruising slowly up and down. Then my father's boat turned toward the dock. It was several feet away and moving. I jumped for it and fell in the bottom, nearly breaking my neck.

"You were supposed to wait till I stopped!" he said. He had only been making a practice run.

It was like him to be making a practice run. No one else had felt the need to. He wanted to make sure.

My brother and I grew bored with Sundays at the Yacht Club. It was as dull as church, put-putting around Kingston Harbour in his motor-boat. The only good thing was that it didn't go on too long.

But he had a better idea. Some of the members had bought cabin cruisers. The rage now was all for cabin cruisers. But instead of buying a cabin cruiser or having one made along the usual lines, my father decided to build one to his own design. He managed to get hold of a lifeboat somewhere. He got an engine somewhere else. He built a cabin in the middle of the boat, square up and down. When, after some months, the cruiser slid down the runway and floated, it looked like something between sea and land, a kind of water-going tram. Needless to say, it ran with relentless efficiency, at a slow rate. He would spend hours going out to Port Royal in the morning and coming back.

The garden-boy was now serving as an able seaman. But my father ran the engine himself. Also, he did not trust anyone else with the wheel, and there was nothing for the rest of us to do but sit on the benches along the sides, like school-benches, and watch the shorelines sliding by. If I kept my eyes fixed on the roof of a house I could see that we were actually moving.

Sometimes a school of porpoises broke the surface. Once or twice we saw the fin of a shark.

When we got to Port Royal the waves from the open sea made the boat roll to and fro. He steered closer to shore. There were pelicans on the posts, and we could see the streets of Port Royal—tumble-down shacks where there had once been a town. The old town had been sunk in an earthquake and tidal wave—it was lying under the waves, deep down, with all the treasure that the pirates had taken from the Spaniards. We looked down into the murky water but couldn't see anything—not a gleam of pirate gold.

I saw a cigar-shaped shadow on the bottom, and, moving my gaze upward, made out the shape of a barracuda, hanging motionless between the shadow and the surface, with its eye fixed steadily upon mine.

We steered close to Fort Charles, where Nelson as a young naval officer had paced up and down, gazing out to sea, yearning to be off to the Nile and Trafalgar. We looked at the lighthouse, then turned back, making the tedious journey over the harbour to the Yacht Club. The sun at noon beat down and the hills beyond Kingston shimmered in the heat. The wake we left behind us was straight as a ruler. I listened for the chords of music that were playing under the monotonous engine sound.

When there was a ship in the harbour—a tanker or one of the white Grace Line steamers—we would go around it. Once there was a big ocean liner, the *Empress of Britain*. Sometimes—and this made me forget the dreary expeditions—there would be a British or American warship with its turrets, great guns and seaplane hoisted on the catapult. Once, as in a dream, I saw the battle-cruiser *Rodney*.

If we went in the other direction, to the east end of the harbour, there would be a seaplane, one of the Pan-American clippers, resting on the water like a white bird. It had flown all the way from America, flying across the sea. This was as hard to believe as stories about dragons.

VI

From going so often to the sea my father had the idea of living near it. One day I went with him—Herbert was not with me, as he was away at school—to look at a house he was thinking of buying. This was near Bournemouth. We walked through the front door and found no one there. Planks and wood-shavings were scattered about. There were holes in the floor and empty cans of paint. Everything was being done at once and nothing was finished.

We were standing in a space that he said was to be the dining-room, when my mother appeared. She stood in the

37

doorway without moving, then she took a step into the room and raised her hand and pointed it at my father. Her hand was holding a revolver. Seconds passed while my heart beat wildly. Then my father moved—he walked across the floor toward her, saying, "Now, Rosalind!" He put his hand on the barrel of the gun and started to take it away. She let it go. Then she uttered a scream and fell to the floor. She lay on her back, rigid, the cords of her neck standing out. Her face was white and bubbles of froth appeared at the corners of her mouth.

After a while he lifted her up and carried her to the car. He placed her on the seat between us, and we drove back to town. She was moaning, her eyes turned back in her head so that only the whites showed. When we came to Cross Roads he told me to get out and walk the short distance home. Then the car drove away.

VII

The day came that I was to go to boarding-school with my brother. A big yellow Buick touring car turned into the driveway. The driver strapped our suitcases on to the luggage-carrier. We got into the car. It was filled with boys of all sizes. One of them said to my brother, "What's his name?"

"Simpson Two," said my brother.

We drove to Halfway Tree, where there was a tower with four clock faces. Then we turned west on a road where, from time to time, a huddle of shacks and shops appeared, to be snatched away behind. The car drove faster and faster. We were on the Spanish Town road, straight and flat between fields of sugar-cane. On the left a train was travelling, belching smoke. There were white, hump-backed cattle and stacks of logwood in the fields. We drove through a narrow street of shacks pressing close together. There was the smell of a Chinaman's shop, kerosene oil and salt fish. Black children, clothed to the waist and naked beneath, stared from the side of the road.

My companions shouted the school song: "Hillcastle! Hillcastle!"

We were climbing into green hills. Mandeville, a little town of white houses and rose gardens, where English people lived. . . .

Then we were descending by hairpin turns in clouds of dust. Then climbing again, into more hills. My companions were smoking. One of them got sick and vomited inside the car, on the floor. The driver stopped and tried to clean it out. Then we started again and kept going up, around hairpin turns. There were john crows flying below us. The air became noticeably cooler.

A long wall of stones lay ahead. We passed through the gate, and there was a driveway lined with willows. This curved to the right, to a chapel and a sprawling two-story building with a red roof. This was Hillcastle, where I would stay for eight years—an eternity, with vacations at Christmas, Easter, and in the summer.

New boys reported to the matron, who assigned them to a dormitory. I was in C Dormitory. It contained twenty beds, each with its own chamber-pot made of tin with white enamel. At each end of the room there was a washstand with pitchers and basins. The roof was supported by square wooden beams.

The dormitory filled up with boys. They greeted each other with shouts. They had all done wonderful things in

39

the holidays. The new boys sat on their beds, a race apart, trying not to be seen.

"Stand up," said a big boy. "What's your name?"

"Simpson Two."

"What form are you in?"

"I don't know."

He pushed me in the chest. I staggered back and fell over another boy who had placed himself on all fours behind me.

When I got to my feet, two other big boys came up, with a small boy between them.

"He says he's a Canadian," they explained to the boy who had pushed me.

He turned to me. "Can you lick a Canadian?"

I didn't know what he meant, but then someone shouted, "Simpson Two is going to fight the Canadian," and more boys came up and formed a circle. They pushed me in the back and I bumped into the Canadian. He had a pleasant, friendly face, round and freckled, with short, blond hair. He hit me in the eye.

I punched him in the chest. Then we were rolling on the floor. In a while I managed to get an arm around his neck, and squeezed. We were both exhausted. We lay there smelling each other.

Then the circle of boys went away, and when I looked up a man was standing there. It was one of the masters. I scrambled to my feet. He looked at us silently, then went away.

A big bell rang, and everyone ran downstairs. It was supper time and we gathered outside the dining-room, "under the arches". The main building was supported by an old-fashioned archway. Bats were flying about, making a squeaking noise.

A handbell rang, and we went into the dining-room. I was in Coke House, so I sat at a long table with the other Coke House boys. I would be eating with them as long as

I was at Hillcastle. At the end of the table sat our house-master, Mister Powell.

Mister Dickson the headmaster appeared at dinner on the first night of term and other important occasions. He was a fat man with a yellow moustache and glasses. He rapped his spoon on the table. Everyone stood up, and one of the long benches fell over. This often happened, I would discover later, and whenever it did the master who was about to say grace would keep us standing in silence, to show his disapproval.

This evening the headmaster himself said grace. "For what we are about to receive may the Lord make us truly thankful."

Then we sat down, and Mister Powell chatted to the boys around him as he helped meat from a bowl into the plates beside him. Tonight it was corned beef and cabbage. The plates were passed down the table, and we helped ourselves to rice and mashed potatoes from the bowls set in the middle. Mister Powell laughed a lot, showing his teeth, and talked about what he had done during the holidays.

In the years to come I would discover that everyone always said they had had a wonderful time during the holidays. The luckiest boys were those who lived in town, Kingston, Montego Bay, or Port Antonio, and the most unfortunate were those who lived in the country and never got to go to movies. There were even a few boys whose homes were not far from the school. What they did during the holidays we could not imagine, and they were too ashamed to speak of it.

*

On this first night, as there was no homework—but they weren't home, so they called it Prep—the boys walked up and down on the barbeque with their friends in twos and

41

threes. The new boys walked up and down too, pretending they had friends. The barbeque was a square paved with concrete around which the buildings were situated. At the far, southern side the barbeque ended at a wall. Standing by the wall, looking down, you saw the hill sloping to the football fields, then the mountain fell away again, a greater distance, till it came to a wide plain. To the right, at the periphery, was a town named Black River. The river itself was said to be full of alligators. It went winding through the marshes, and a cape like a lizard projected into the sea. In front the horizon was unbroken sea and clouds, now rayed with the light of the setting sun. At nightfall lights began to shine from Black River, but most of the people who lived down there on the plain had no lights and lived in darkness.

The bell rang, and everyone went to chapel. On the first night the masters and boys sang loudly, and Mister Wiehen at the organ pulled out the stops so that the walls seemed to shake, though they were made of stone.

> He who would valiant be
> 'Gainst all disaster,
> Let him in constancy
> Follow the master.
> There's no discouragement
> Shall make him once relent
> His first avowed intent
> To be a pilgrim.

They trooped out of chapel to the dormitories. In a few minutes they were in bed and it was "lights out".

I lay in bed on this, my first night at school, feeling the rough sheets and listening to the noises the boys made as they settled to sleep. There was whispering and the flicker of a candle. Then "Hush!" and the candle went out. Someone stood in the doorway—one of the masters. They would give you a licking if they caught you out of bed or

talking. Or else they would give you five hundred lines.
He went away and the boys listened to his steps retreating.
Outside the wind was blowing in gusts so that the roof
creaked on the beams. The night was colder than at home
and I was glad of my blanket. We never had to use a
blanket at home. A light came through windows from the
moon scudding through clouds. They said that if you had
to get up at night and go to the toilet, which was in another
building some distance away, you would meet the Rolling
Calf. The Rolling Calf had eyes as big as plates, shining like
automobile headlights, and it came rolling toward you,
roaring as it came.

But then you were asleep.

VIII

First Bell was at six. You didn't have to get up—there were
a few boys, however, who went running to the showers,
across the barbeque, in bare feet and naked except for a
towel. These were the sportsmaster's pets, the runners and
players of football and cricket. There were also a few early
risers who had to do lines: they had to write maybe a
thousand times, in clear handwriting on lined sheets of
foolscap, "I shall not disturb the class by talking." There
were one or two boys who got up early to snatch a few
blessed minutes when the world had not yet burst in, shouting and interfering. They pasted stamps in an album, or
turned the pages of a book. *Chums*, the red annual with
stories about English boarding-schools, the Foreign Legion,

fighting on the Western Front, racing-car drivers and explorers . . .

At Second Bell everyone had to get up. The first ones at the wash-stands got plenty of water. Those who rose last found only an inch in the pitcher, not enough water to clean the accumulated scum out of the basin. Then everyone out! to the dining-room, for a cup of hot cocoa and a slice of bread with margarine. This was real margarine, not one of your substitutes for butter. It was white and rancid, straight from the locomotive shed, and it had one advantage—it killed the weevils in the slice of bread, and if it failed to kill them, bogged them down so that they could not be seen moving.

There was an hour of morning Prep, then chapel—a piece of Scripture, a psalm, a hymn, and two prayers. Then breakfast, and after breakfast, classes.

Form Two, in which I began, was the lowest. The forms were numbered up to Six, where the prefects were. Every number was divided into a lower form and an upper, B and A, so that the years were a series of downs and ups, a year of obscurity to be followed by a year of light. It seemed that the rooms for the lower forms were cramped and uncomfortable, your desk pushed in a corner, and it was then that the miserable things happened. It was in IIIB that I always seemed to be greasing the football-players' boots and shining their shoes—and it was when I was in IIIB that I looked through the Sixth Form window.

"Come here, boy," said Weller. He was big, about six feet tall. "What you looking in the Sixth Form window for?"

The Sixth Form boys lined up in two rows facing each other. Weller put me at the far end, looking down the rows. Some of the boys seemed sheepish—they didn't enjoy these occasions as much as Weller did. I was given a push forward, and after that I didn't have to walk or run—I was propelled by one kick after another so that I went flying to the door. The last kick was the worst, from Weller with the point of his shoe. I picked myself off the concrete and limped away.

In IIIA, on the other hand, I found a friend—Peter Lopez. Peter was my trains and boxing friend. Pacing the barbeque from the main building to the wall and back again, we talked about these matters. Peter liked *The Flying Scotsman* while I liked *The Royal Scot*. We talked the great fights again—Corbett–Fitzimmons, Dempsey versus Tunney. I was for Dempsey and thought he had been cheated by the "fourteen count".

I also had a friend named Beverly Dodd, who stuttered. Beverly was my reading friend—we read novels and passed them to each other. *Bulldog Drummond. The Scarlet Pimpernel. The Thirty-Nine Steps.*

But IVB, again, was a time of darkness. It was during this year that the bell tolled in the middle of the day and the school assembled in the hall in the main building. What was happening? No one knew.

The headmaster, Mister Dickson, entered. He had a cane under his arm. He stood on the platform facing us. He was fat and had a drooping, yellow moustache; his eyes were sunk in fat and concealed by the glint of his spectacles. He read a list of names—"Forsyth, Mair I, Cargyll". I saw these boys go up to the platform, snatched from our very midst. Then the headmaster called for four of the prefects to come up. He told them to move a table to the middle of the platform. He told Mair I to lie face down on the table, and told the prefects to hold him by his arms and legs. Then he stepped forward and brought the cane down with all his strength on the boy's back. He brought it down six times, and each time the body on the table stiffened. Then he said "Get up!" and Mair I got to his feet and walked off the platform. He was moving with difficulty, but he had not uttered a sound.

45

The same for Forsyth and Cargyll.

We watched this execution in silence. Every cut of the stick seemed to bite into our flesh. When the headmaster had finished beating the three boys, he announced that they had been swimming in the water-tank. This was one of the worst, almost unheard-of, offences. It was nearly as bad as being caught smoking, or going out-of-bounds, over the school wall, for which there was an even greater punishment—being expelled. If you were expelled your life would be ruined.

*

Yet, underneath this regime we developed a life of our own. Then, everybody had his speciality, a game he could play or thing he could make, and some had a moment of glory. I too had mine and it came unexpectedly.

We ate our meals at long tables, sitting in two rows with a master at the head of the table. We were allowed to ask for "seconds" by passing our empty plates up to the master, who would serve meat from the dish in front of him. As I've said, we were badly fed; we had plenty of fresh fruit, oranges and mangoes, but the rest was yam and rice, meat that was sometimes rotten, bread with weevils in it. But we had to eat, and sometimes we asked for seconds.

One evening I passed up my plate for a second helping of pork—gobbets of fat swimming in gravy. You were supposed just to pass your plate without saying anything, but I said "Meat please!" The boy sitting next to me, as he passed my plate, also said "Meat please!" I hadn't thought he would—I'd meant it only as a joke between the two of us. Or had I? As my plate made its way to the end of the table so did the whisper, increasing in sarcasm. I would have done anything to call back the plate, but it went tilting on its way, increasing in velocity as though it had a will of its own and

had been waiting for this release, saying "Meat please!"
Heads turned toward me, then the master stared down the
table. It was obvious that I was guilty—I was the one who
had no plate in front of him. "There are some small boys..."
the master began, in a cracked voice. I did not hear what he
said—I was stunned. But I knew that it was loud and the
whole school was listening.

Afterwards I was slapped on the back and congratulated—
not least by the boys who, by passing on the words, had got
me into that fix. I hadn't really intended, except for the
fraction of a moment, to rebel; but perhaps this is the way
rebellions start. You throw yourself forward on an impulse,
then find you must abide the consequences.

As we couldn't fight back, we learned how to cheat. One
day we were taking an exam in hygiene and the master left
the room for an hour. Immediately all the desks flew open
and we copied the answers out of the textbook. This was
incredibly naïve, and the next day the frightful rumour flew
round that the master was going to call us in to explain our
answers. I sat down and memorized the relevant pages.
When it was my turn to go in and see the master I was able
to recite the text word for word. He let me go without
making any comment. He too must have been remarkably
naïve, for he might simply have asked me a question that
would have required a word-for-word knowledge of some
other part of the text. To this day I can remember the words
of one answer, concerning the ability of an English family
in reduced circumstances, living in the Midlands, to support
itself "by ringing the changes on pease and beans".

Much of our education was of this kind. It was assumed
that we would be living in England and no attempt was
made to translate what we learned into Jamaican. So we
learned how to keep warm in Birmingham in the winter,
and where coal was mined, and how English children went
to look at the Changing of the Guard. We were being fitted

47

for a life that we would never have and being made to understand that the life we did have was inferior.

And of course there was no place in the classroom for "bad English"—that is, Jamaican words and expressions. The most important weapon of a ruling class is language, which controls everything. The native language must be suppressed so that the natives cannot communicate with one another directly but only through their masters.

Am I making too much of the life of schoolboys? Hillcastle was an epitome of Jamaica; it was there we developed a colonial mentality.

As Jamaicans did not govern themselves they felt inferior in other respects. "Among the legacies of a colonial culture is the habit of thinking of creative sources as somehow remote from itself." This was true of the Jamaicans.

They were only a remote branch of England. They were not self-sufficient, and had created no important works. The history of Jamaica was the history of the Europeans who had ruled it, and there were no native heroes who might be mentioned in the same breath with Nelson. Jamaicans might become lawyers and doctors, but this would be only a kind of play-acting, for the centres of law and medicine were thousands of miles away. The very trees and hills of Jamaica were only a kind of papiermâché—the famous landscapes were in England. No Jamaican bird could sing like Keats' nightingale, and Jamaican flowers were not as beautiful as Wordsworth's daffodils.

★

But when I was promoted to Form IVA the time was again filled with light. It was then that I wrote an essay on the coronation of George VI that won a prize and was printed in *The Daily Gleaner*, the newspaper published in Kingston. Years later I came across a letter that my father wrote to my mother on this occasion. She was living in Toronto, Canada, working for a firm that sold cosmetics. He had taken the trouble to write: "See what the boy has done."

I had copied a circumstantial account of the coronation from an article in the *Gleaner*, selecting the more colourful episodes—as perhaps the writer in the *Gleaner* had taken his account from a London newspaper. I began by comparing London to a bee-hive. I showed the procession of men and horses. I added touches of my own, quoting Gray:

> Girt with many a Baron bold
> Sublime their starry fronts they rear;
> And gorgeous Dames, and Statesmen old
> In bearded majesty, appear.

I also quoted Shakespeare, who had said discouraging things about the burden of wearing a crown, and rebuked him for not sufficiently respecting the royal family, our king, our queen, and their children. Shakespeare, I thought, could stand it; he could afford to be dispraised, and at this point finding fault with him gave a fillip to my essay, which was threatening to be just a description. An argument between Shakespeare and myself should hold the reader in suspense.

First prize. Five pounds. L. A. M. Simpson. Age 14.

With this, the first money I had earned, and the most I had ever held in my hand—five pounds, a fortune!—I bought a bicycle. This was during the holidays, and my stepmother watched me learning to ride.

"You're a clever boy," she said. "Your father's very proud of you. If only your brother would work harder and not make his father angry."

IX

For my father had married again. I received the announcement one night at school. Around me boys were bending over their books, in the room that shone like a lighted box. They were doing sums, but I was trying to penetrate a mystery of human behaviour.

"She's attractive," my father wrote, "and I'm sure you'll love her. She has red hair, like Clara Bow."

I was surprised, and had a peculiar feeling, like shame. It made me feel embarrassed to see my father thinking about a woman. I had never heard him speak of the relations between men and women, yet now it seemed that he had been strongly attracted. By red hair.

Clara Bow was a motion-picture actress. No doubt he'd been trying to think of some way to recommend his new wife to his children. Then he hit upon the solution: he knew that we liked movies. His wife had red hair, like Clara Bow in the movies. Therefore we would love our stepmother. That it might be in poor taste to recommend, in terms of physical attractiveness, the woman he had chosen to replace our mother, did not enter our father's head. Such sensitivity as he possessed—and it had never been much—had been exhausted in the law courts.

When he was a young man, in his bachelor days, he had let himself dream. There were books of adventure in his study, worm-eaten, tunnelled through and through, and a powder fell out when you opened them—tales of voyages up the Orinoco and African explorations. They were illustrated with pictures of wild animals—jaguar, buffalo, crocodile—and pictures of savages and bearded men with rifles.

In his office, framed on a wall, were some lines of poetry showing that he'd once meditated on the theme of love.

> The night has a thousand eyes,
>   And the day but one;
> Yet the light of the bright world dies
>   With the dying sun.
>
> The mind has a thousand eyes,
>   And the heart but one;
> Yet the light of a whole life dies
>   When love is done.

This poem mystified me every time I saw it. It hinted at a side of my father I had never seen—sad and, had I known the word, sentimental. It haunts me to this day—I want to say to him: Don't you see what bad poetry it is? What eyes can the brain have? Or the heart? And in any case, if the brain has a thousand eyes, whatever this means, why shouldn't the heart have a thousand, too?

But he looks at me in a puzzled manner. He doesn't know what I'm talking about. It's not supposed to make sense, it's only a poem, that he hung up long ago. That was when he was a bachelor, before he married.

The only thing you can depend on is intelligence and hard work. All this thinking about love is nonsense—making a lot of trouble for people.

*

He had made a new life for himself, rearranging every-thing after the confusion of the divorce. He had married again and bought a new house. He devoted himself entirely to his work and stayed home with his wife. He no longer went into society or invited friends to his home.

He was worried about Herbert, however. Herbert, having left school, was now at the office, studying law. But he wasn't passing his exams—this was what my stepmother meant. Herbert sat staring at the pages of law, but he was day-dreaming. His only enthusiasm was for Physical Culture—he subscribed to Bernarr Macfadden's magazine, and studied photographs of men with bulging biceps and triceps and ridged stomach muscles, in statuesque poses. He exercised morning and night. He was becoming more and more muscular. The mornings long ago when he had stood in front of the Victrola, with his mother and father, doing exercises to the sound of music, were having this result. Then he had been happy, when to touch his toes twelve times in succession had brought an approving smile to his father's countenance.

Also, Herbert boxed—and his father, no doubt hoping that if he encouraged Herbert in this foolishness, out of gratitude he would become a brilliant lawyer, went so far as to hire a prize-fighter, an old welterweight named McVey, who came every week and gave us boxing lessons. I say "us" because for some reason it was assumed that I wanted to box too. I could if I had to, but I preferred swimming.

And my bicycle . . . I took long rides in the afternoon, through the lanes of Kingston, and sometimes as far as the Manor House Hotel at Constant Springs. This was where we stayed on the occasions when our mother came back to the island. She visited sometimes for a few weeks in the summer, and my brother and I would stay with her.

The hotel was a rambling structure with long verandas, surrounded with green lawns and beds of flowers. We were close to the hills. They shone like crystal in the dewy atmosphere. There were tennis courts and a golf course. At times it seemed that my mother, Herbert and I were the only guests—except for an English couple who kept to themselves, only saying "Good morning" in the polite, dismissive English way as they took their place at the breakfast table. And an American businessman, reading his home-town paper. I could not make sense of American newswriting—it seemed like a foreign language.

Then our mother would go back to Canada, and we went back to our father's house. This was at Bournemouth—a new house, right on the harbour, with its own beach. His boat lay tied securely to the dock.

X

Aunt Ethel said, "Aston married her for her legs."

But this did not have the effect my aunt intended, to paint an erotic picture. Separating my stepmother's legs from the rest of her body made me think of a museum where the parts of ancient statues are kept in glass cases— here an arm, there a leg. I thought of my father not as driven by passion, but by curiosity. Perhaps he had wished to possess my stepmother's legs, but this was a failing for which one could not help having a certain admiration—as one would for a man so curious about statues that he took them out of the museum and carried them home to study them at his leisure.

It seemed, indeed, that my father had been taken out of the usual course of his life by a feeling he could not entirely control. With a touching eagerness to have us co-operate, he said to my brother and myself that we would have to find a name for our stepmother—we couldn't call her mother, or Elizabeth, as he did. We ought to call her by some sort of nickname, the kind of name that would be thought up by stepchildren for a stepmother of whom they had grown fond. Bitsy! That was it. We were to call her Bitsy from now on.

It must have struck our stepmother as odd to be called by a name she had never heard before, but no doubt our father explained to her that my brother and myself had grown so fond of her that we were impelled suddenly to call her Bitsy. He liked to have a clear understanding all around.

Nevertheless, I became fond of Bitsy on my own account. In the first year of marriage she was making an effort to be nice to her stepchildren. I was grateful to her for being kind, but I was more grateful to her for being a woman. It had been a long time since I had been included in the atmosphere a man and woman living together generate round them. There was an exciting warmth in the house—opposite to the drab piety in the house of Uncle Percy and my aunts. And compared to boarding-school it was pure magic.

I brooded over the Montgomery Ward catalogue with Bitsy. Which glider should she get for the veranda? The one with green and white stripes, or the one that came apart in sections? And would it be here in time for Christmas? Together we studied the pictures of red barns, silos, and tractors with huge tyres. There was a boy in boots trudging over the landscape and pulling a little wagon behind him. What a strange place America was!

Then she turned to the women's foundation garments. Stout women, middle-sized women, slender women. And women's underwear—there were beautiful girls with blonde, brunette and red hair, all lined up for inspection and practically naked. Others were in pyjamas. I was blushing furiously.

"Isn't that a pretty one?" Bitsy said, pointing to a picture. Soon after this I found a reason to excuse myself and left. I was shocked. I had not imagined women pointing out such things to a member of the opposite sex.

At the end of the year Bitsy gave birth, and if the atmosphere of the house had been feminine, now it was maternal. There were diapers on lines and a smell of warm mash, baby powder and urine. One day, I came upon Bitsy in, of all places, my father's study, with a breast exposed. The baby was clamped on to it by the mouth. Bitsy did not seem disturbed by my presence, nor did she make an attempt to cover herself. I backed rapidly out of the room. Another shock.

When the baby was old enough to be taken outside, I accompanied Bitsy as she wheeled the carriage down to the beach. We sat for an hour and watched the waves breaking. The trailing smoke of a ship passed across the sky, on the other side of the Palisadoes. My father's boat lay anchored at bow and stern and roped to the dock fore and aft, so that nothing short of a hurricane could tear it loose; the hull gave off a cheerful, slapping sound.

It was almost as though I had a family of my own.

XI

H. J. Andrews had been hired from Scotland to teach us English. He was round-shouldered and peered through glasses with thick lenses. He would open the book and ask us to read aloud in turn.

> I know you all, and will awhile uphold
> The unyoked humour of your idleness.
> Yet herein will I imitate the sun,

Who doth permit the base contagious clouds
To smother up his beauty from the world,
That when he please again to be himself,
Being wanted he may be more wond'red at,
By breaking through the foul and ugly mists
Of vapours that did seem to strangle him.
If all the year were playing holidays,
To sport would be as tedious as to work;
But when they seldom come, they wished for come,
And nothing pleaseth but rare accidents:
So, when this loose behaviour I throw off,
And pay the debt I never promised,
By how much better than my word I am,
By so much shall I falsify men's hopes,
And like bright metal on a sullen ground,
My reformation, glitt'ring o'er my fault,
Shall show more goodly, and attract more eyes,
Than that which hath no foil to set it off.
I'll so offend, to make offence a skill,
Redeeming time when men think least I will.

He spoke of the character of the prince. Hal was a brave soldier and, in spite of appearances, a dutiful son. He would be the hero of Agincourt and an efficient king. As this speech proved, he was level-headed, foresighted, calculating. You might call him a hypocrite.

We shall find a similar character in *Antony and Cleopatra*— Augustus, whom Shakespeare opposes to Mark Antony. Augustus, also, is calculating and efficient, and he defeats Antony, as Prince Hal defeats Harry Hotspur. But the question arises: what do these calculating people win? And isn't there something about the character of an Antony or Hotspur or Falstaff that makes us prefer them to the hero with all his victories?

This is not to say that Shakespeare wishes to show the

prince in a bad light. To the contrary, he is presenting the model of what a king has to be. But, at the same time, because he is a poet he cannot falsify life—just as people who have no poetry in them never manage to see life as it is.

Let us consider the character of Falstaff, this wine-bibber, this tub of lard, this coward . . . well, is Falstaff a coward? Mair II?

Yes, sir, he won't fight.

And a good thing too! If Falstaff had tried to tackle Hotspur he would have been carved up in fat little pieces. And notice, on Gadshill, Falstaff *does* fight—for a while, before he takes to his heels. Is that the action of a coward?

But sir, he's always bragging. And he's a liar.

Is he? Do you suppose for a moment that Falstaff expects to be believed? Don't you see what he's doing? "I am not witty in myself, but the cause that wit is in other men." The lies Falstaff tells are not meant to be believed—they are meant to be found out. See how the others egg him on, to tell bigger and bigger lies, and see how he obliges them. Do you imagine that Falstaff isn't aware that you can't see colours in the dark, and that he has upped the number of men in buckram from one line to another? No, obviously it's for the purpose of making people laugh, to make them come alive. Prince Hal seems alive only when he is with Falstaff.

So I was shown for the first time that literature is a reflection of life rather than a bundle of clichés. Shakespeare was creating characters out of life, not cardboard figures of virtue and vice.

Then we read *Macbeth* and *The Tempest*, and by this time it was all over with me—I would be attached to poetry for the rest of my life. The ground I walked on seemed no more solid than the imaginary green fields of England and the moors of Scotland. I could believe with Prospero that the great globe itself was a dream. In which case, the poets who dreamed so well made better worlds, for they did not fade.

I began sending my pocket-money to England for books. *Vanity Fair* was said to be a great novel; moreover, it had a description of the battle of Waterloo. Ever since early childhood, when I saw a movie about it, I had been fascinated with Waterloo. I would have been on the French side, in the cavalry that Ney launched again and again at the British squares—it was more romantic. So I sent a postal money order to London for *Vanity Fair*. It took two months for the book to arrive. I read it in a corner of a classroom while around me boys were shooting wads of paper at each other with rubber bands. I took my book out under the willows, with clouds streaming over. This was the first "classic" I read on my own account and not as a school assignment. I read every word and finished with a sense of triumph.

Then I read Dickens, and novels by Austen, Hardy, and Conrad. I was reading not because I had to, but because it was a pleasure, and as I read I became filled with a desire to write. I wanted to tell stories and write poems of my own. Perhaps to be admired—but more important, because there were things I had seen and felt that I wanted other people to see and feel.

I had a talent for writing essays. These were set every week, and I would cheerfully have written on any subject.

I tried my hand at a story. *The Daily Gleaner*, where I had been awarded a prize for my coronation essay, was now holding a short-story competition. I wrote a story about a poor country boy who went to Kingston and was involved in an earthquake. (I had an uncle who had lost a leg in an earthquake and was nicknamed "Corkfoot". Besides, I had seen an earthquake in the movie *San Francisco*.) In my story one of the earthquake victims, as he lay dying, gave the hero a wallet full of money. The country boy returned to his village; but he found his old mother dying, and the last words of the story were, "Too late! Too late!"

This, too, won a prize and was published in *The Gleaner*.

In bed at night, in the row of sleeping boys, I would lie listening to the wind that roared across the commons, making the roof creak like a ship. I was envisioning cities, battles, and beautiful women, and my adventures were always taking place across the sea—in England or France.

XII

During the holidays I went swimming at Bournemouth, right down the street from our house. On week-days I had the pool pretty much to myself and lay for hours reading and looking at the white caps driving across the harbour. But on Saturdays and Sundays the pool filled up with people; you could hear them shouting a long way off.

One Saturday when I came out of the locker-room I found myself face to face with grey eyes, a fine nose, long bright hair. This vision also had a body, slenderly curving. She passed me with a steady gaze, looking into my eyes, and when she had gone by, in the rear of her bathing-suit there was a moth hole as big as a threepence.

She played in the pool, throwing the ball to her young brother. I found a way to speak to him, and learned his name and that of his sister. I became friends with him, and urged him to come swimming often and bring his sister with him.

When I plucked up courage to speak to her she must have known by my awkwardness how I felt. Though she came to Bournemouth several times I remained just as tongue-tied. But at night in my thoughts before sleep it was another matter. There I spoke and acted well and she looked at me with admiration.

I persuaded her brother to come to a movie with me and bring her along. This was at the Carib Theatre, the new movie-house at Cross Roads in comparison with which everything else of the kind paled into insignificance. I waited outside, and at last they got off a tram. She was wearing her school uniform and a crucifix on a chain down her neck.

They were playing *The Firefly*. I thought that the girl sitting beside me was like the woman in the picture. We were living in Spain and listening to wonderful music.

I was always thinking about her. I had great plans. I would do . . . what? Nothing in particular, and everything. I was drawn out of my body and seemed to walk on air. Knowing that she lived on a certain street made it a dangerous place, and when I came near on my bicycle my pulse beat faster and my legs were weak. Suppose she came out and we met! But she never did, and I saw her only when she came to the pool.

She is a figure painted by Botticelli, against a seascape with clouds and palms. The bathing-suit that grips her slenderness is old and worn, and has moth-holes in it, one to the side and one behind, so that her skin shines through. Her hair is long and comes down her back. Her eyes are grey and gentle. She has a soft voice, speaking the Jamaican way—in a kind of sing-song, mistaking the vowels and accents.

When I went back to school I dreamed of her and talked of her continually to my friend Peter. At this time it seemed I could do nothing wrong, either at work or play.

> The isle is full of noises,
> Sounds and sweet airs that give delight and hurt not.

I applied myself to my books and went in for sports with a light heart. On the rifle range the bull sat on my front sight without wavering. I practised on the bar and rings in the gymnasium, and was the best boxer in my weight.

The external world was changing as though in sympathy with my feelings. The mad old headmaster fell sick, and the boys, who were not sentimental, strummed their ukeleles, singing "I'll be glad when you're dead, you rascal you!" He did die, and a new headmaster came from Canada. He set about improving the school. He cut down the flogging and bullying, though not entirely, and gave the bigger boys a taste of freedom. We were allowed to stay up an extra hour after lights-out, and athletics were no longer compulsory.

So when other boys were playing cricket I would lie under the willows, gorging on poetry and novels. Wind sighed in the leaves, and shadows of branches and clouds flitted over the page.

> On Wenlock Edge the wood's in trouble;
>   His forest fleece the Wrekin heaves;
> The gale, it plies the saplings double,
> And thick on Severn snow the leaves.

Or I would be reading *The Dynasts*.

> By degrees the fog lifts, and the Plain is disclosed. From this elevation, gazing north, the expanse looks like the palm of a monstrous right hand, a little hollowed, some half-dozen miles across, wherein the ball of the thumb is roughly represented by heights to the east, on which the French centre has gathered . . .

There were also poems by T. S. Eliot. I could not make sense of them, yet I was haunted by the images and the music of the lines.

> I will show you something different from either
> Your shadow at morning striding behind you

61

Or your shadow at evening rising to meet you;
I will show you fear in a handful of dust.

The new headmaster introduced us to such esoteric
material as the writings of Aldous Huxley. We had discussions of Huxley's *Ends and Means*, during which we
considered what he meant by non-attachment. They were
like the discussions that prefects had with their headmaster
at the better English schools. Sometimes the headmaster
would tell jokes from *Punch*, and we laughed at these in a
sophisticated way. I do not wish to be ungrateful to Mr.
Gordon, but I have wondered whether these man-to-man
talks, when the man is thirty and the boy is sixteen, are not
more damaging in the long run than the brutality of the old
system. Under the old regime we had known what masters
were and what we were—there was no confusion of our
attitudes. They were the enemy, and we had a code of our
own, our own friends and beliefs. But under Mr. Gordon's
enlightened regime we were being absorbed into the
Establishment. We were learning the attitudes of the English
ruling class. We were learning that we were superior and
that many things were ridiculous. German seriousness was
ridiculous; French frivolity was ridiculous; Americans with
their devotion to the dollar were ridiculous. The only people
who were not ridiculous were those who had gone to a
British public school and were going to Oxford or
Cambridge.

We were learning English manners. But there was a catch
—Jamaicans were not Englishmen and never could be, even
the few who would go to English universities. I was beginning to see the paradox, the fundamental contradiction that
made it impossible for the Empire to continue. The English
were always educating people beyond their place in the class
system. Then the young men came up against class barriers
and were frustrated. So they became rebels, educated ones,

and set about driving out the English. At a later time a similar situation would come about in England itself. Young Englishmen from lower-class families were educated beyond their class at the red-brick universities. Then they came up against class barriers and were "angry young men", fulminating against the system.

XIII

Everyone was singing "Stormy Weather". Gales knocked down the banana trees, drove flat swathes through the sugar-cane, and tore the roofs off houses and sent them flying. At last came a hurricane and a flood that poured down the gullies, carrying away the shacks that people had built on the gully beds. A number of drowned bodies, with the carcasses of mules, pigs, and chickens, were floating on the sea. The sharks had a feast. For weeks the sea kept rejecting these gifts, casting them back, shark-bitten and the worse for wear, on to the beach.

Herbert and I baited a hook with a lump of pork and caught a shark. We hauled it on to the beach and stood, taking care not to get close to its teeth, pumping bullets into its head from a rifle. The bullets merely disappeared, and at last when the shark expired it was of suffocation.

A cadaver with naked feet, in a white shirt and trousers, floated down to our fence where it was caught, and when the water subsided the dead man lay in the mud. Long after the body had been removed, on nights when I would be walking home from the tram, with the movie I had been to running through my head, as I approached our house I would see the hollow filled with lamplight in the shape of a man lying close to the gate.

A light was on in my father's study. Working late on his cases. . . . And a light in the bedroom I shared with my brother. He too would be working.

Herbert had again failed his law exams. What obstinacy! Every morning my father set out for the office with Herbert. They left in silence. What could they have had to say to each other on those rides? Herbert had failed his exams again and again. Was he trying to make a laughing-stock of his father? How could the most famous defence counsel on the island have a son who could not pass exams?

For Aston Simpson was famous—everyone knew about his cases. Crown *vs*. Lowy, for example. The case had been reported in England, even in the American newspapers. Mrs. Lowy had gone to bed one night with her husband and waked the next morning to find that he had been shot through the head. The finger of suspicion pointed to the widow, and my father as defence counsel, together with Manley as barrister, undertook to defend her.

Manley's wife was artistic, and they asked her to make a model of the dead man's head in plaster-of-paris. Through this they made a hole with a brass curtain-rod. When the head was brought into court and exhibited to the jury they were astonished. My father passed the curtain-rod through the hole, demonstrating the direction of the bullet, and argued that it must have been fired by someone standing outside the bedroom. A burglar, presumably. The jury returned a verdict of Not Guilty. The plaster-of-paris head was standing in a closet at home. If you opened the door— Bang!—there was the head with a hole through it.

Yet his son could not pass exams!

Anyone could pass if he put his mind to it. Young Nigel, whom my father had taken into his office, was already preparing his finals, and Nigel was the same age as Herbert. Nigel would be a lawyer when his own son was still trying to pass an exam.

When he was a young man he did not have a father with a profession he could inherit. He came down from the country when he was a boy in order to study law, and that was what he had done. No one would have helped him if he had failed, given him food and a roof over his head. Nevertheless, he had made his way, without asking for help from anyone, and today the name Aston Simpson was known throughout the island.

Herbert was obstinate, that was his trouble. It was worse than obstinacy—it was sullenness and ingratitude. He had set himself against his father.

What was that junk Herbert was always reading? Physical Culture! Physical Culture indeed! Was he hoping to earn a living by Physical Culture?

He knew what was at the root of the trouble, and it was no use Herbert's trying to deny it—he resented his stepmother. Well, there'd be a stop to that!

Thus, the ride from the house at Bournemouth to the office on Duke Street. When my father got there he wrote a letter to Herbert's mother, putting the case plainly so that any fool could see it.

Dear Rosalind,

I must ask you again not to put foolish ideas in Herbert's head. He has failed his exams, and he says that you have written to him saying that he may be able to study medicine, and go to McGill in Canada. This is out of the question. Herbert has no ability in that direction, and must persist in the study of law. If he puts aside the foolishness of Physical Culture and boxing and attends to his books, he will pass his exams. In any case he will stay in Jamaica. Your children would not be able to live in

65

Canada or the United States. Let me remind you that they are Jamaican, *with all that this implies!*

I do not know what is wrong with your sons. They are always reading and have no interest in practical things. They have no interest in the motor-boat or the cars. I shall not be here forever to pay for their food and keep a roof over their heads. In any case, I have other obligations.

I am not worried about Louis, however. He will do well—as I told you in my last letter, he came first in the Senior Cambridge and is now working for his Higher Schools Certificate. He will be the first boy at Hillcastle to take this examination in literature rather than science. Of course, he will never be able to argue a case in court, because of his teeth. It was a pity you sent him the skates.

(My father had come to believe—at least, he persisted in declaring—I had broken my teeth while roller-skating. This was not true—I broke them rough-housing with Herbert. He was on all fours and I was on his back; he reared up and I was pitched on to my face, smashing my teeth. Throughout my boyhood I had to wear a gold cap to protect the remnant of a top front tooth. The gold was conspicuous, and I tried to talk without opening my mouth so that no one would notice it.)

But though Louis will not be able to address a jury, I have no doubt that he will make his way as a solicitor.

To return to Herbert—I must ask you not to encourage him in these foolish ideas—about going to Canada and studying medicine. And let me advise you again *not* to fill his head with ideas of a more personal, resentful nature. You are at liberty to think that you have been treated unfairly, but it is foolish to make Herbert think so. I will not tolerate rudeness from Herbert, to *anyone*. He has to live in this house and be on good terms with *everyone* in it.

I am glad to hear that your health has improved and that you are now employed by the firm of Helena Rubinstein. This seems more sensible than your travelling from place to place. "A rolling stone gathers no moss."

I hope that the next time I write to you I shall have better news of Herbert. All that he needs is to get down to work and not have his head filled with *foolish ideas.*

As ever,
Aston

Thus, my father. And therefore Herbert was up late at night, studying Estovers and Emblements, and Contracts and Incorporeal Hereditaments—trying to come to terms with Pledge, Chattel, Mortgage, and Lien—to tell a Malfeasance from a Misfeasance, and a Non-Feasance from either, and to make his peace with Torts.

The situation, hinted at in my father's letter, was that Herbert and his stepmother were no longer on speaking terms, and therefore his father was furious with him.

How had this come about? At the beginning, as I have said, Bitsy had been eager to be nice to her stepchildren. But then she saw that it did not matter—she could please herself. Aston would not find fault with her—at least not on behalf of the children by his first wife. So Bitsy no longer made the effort.

She had a child of her own and was pregnant with another. The children of her husband's first marriage were a nuisance, if not a definite obstacle. She had to think of the future and look out for her children and herself.

On one or two occasions Bitsy was snappish. Herbert, on his side, immediately retired into silence. In a short time they were no longer speaking to each other. Then Bitsy had reason to complain of Herbert to his father, over some matter of household management, and Herbert was given a talking-to. From this time forward he regarded his stepmother as a traitor—not to be trusted. She and his father were in league against him. On their side, they believed that Herbert resented the woman who had taken his mother's place. Herbert's attitude—this was the root of the trouble. They treated him as though he were resentful, and so, of course, he was.

★

On one occasion Herbert wrote a long letter to his stepmother, asking her if their misunderstandings couldn't be patched up; immediately she showed the letter to his father, and he burst in upon us, where we were reading in our bedroom, and launched into a tirade against Herbert, as though he were a criminal in the dock, accusing him of being envious of his little half-sister. Herbert was astonished; he was reduced to silence and an obstinacy which endured for the rest of our lives in that house.

If I seem, in this account, not to have the affection for my father that I should have, there is reason for it. In time he became less like the man we had known when we were small. His humour disappeared, his sarcasms became more frequent, and he was, almost as a policy, unjust to my brother. When Herbert failed his examinations his father treated him with what I can only describe as hatred. On the other hand, I must have been a source of some satisfaction to my father, for I shone at school and, being of a more pliant nature than Herbert, I did not come in for the harsh words to which he was subjected. At times, I was even privileged to have confidential talks with Bitsy. Nevertheless, Herbert was my brother and I was fond of him; we lived together and I suffered from the outbreaks of anger that were directed against him and the coldness in the days that followed.

In recent years my brother has reminded me of the

atmosphere in that house, where he and I were treated like boarders. Our father would go for a walk in the evening with his wife and new child, excluding us, and we were made to feel that it was not our home, but that we were there on sufferance. Our father's behaviour was a demonstration of Rochefoucauld's maxim, that we never forgive those whom we have injured. He had injured our mother, and we were a living reproach. To sum up, this man, who was regarded as one of the best lawyers in Jamaica, was unjust to his own children and behaved in a way a peasant would have been ashamed of. Indeed, there were peasants in Jamaica who were uneducated and had their children out of wedlock, yet treated them with far greater affection than was known in our family.

As I write this account of my father and stepmother, I am aware that there is something "underbred" about it. This is not a dramatic story—there was only bad feeling, day after day. There was in fact something lower-class about these people—and I am using the word deliberately. I have known poor people who are generous—they are the upper class in my opinion—but I would say that my father and his second wife, with all their money, were lower-class, for they had low emotions. They treated themselves well and other people badly.

It is the kind of story you read about in Chekhov, and I think of Chekhov's letter to his brother, where he speaks of their bad upbringing, of "that flesh raised on the rod", the brutalized, inconsiderate life of people who are emotionally or culturally—in the deep sense of the word—illiterate. It is necessary to refine oneself, to lift oneself by one's boot-straps out of the muck of insensitivity. The secret of living well is to treat other people decently, that's all. It was a secret my father never learned, and all my life I have been trying to learn it.

XIV

When I came into the house my father was not in his study. The light came from his bedroom. As I went past the door he said, "Louis?" I knocked and went in.

He was sitting up in bed, with books and papers around him. Bitsy had moved the typewriter into the bedroom, and was taking dictation. On a table by the bed there were bottles of medicine, a glass, and a spoon. He had been ill of late—the doctor had come several times—but he did not let this keep him from going to the office.

"I want to talk to you," he said. Whereupon Bitsy went out of the room.

Against the sheets he looked darker than usual, and somewhat smaller. He peered at me over his glasses. I could not imagine what he wanted to talk about. I was going back to Hillcastle the next day—perhaps he wanted to talk about my schooling.

"Did Bitsy give you your pocket-money?"

I said that she had.

"Well, then, everything seems to be in order."

He paused for a while, then said, "I don't want you to worry. Whatever happens, you'll be well taken care of."

What did he mean? Worry about what? I was embarrassed, as I always was by any attempt on his part to talk of personal matters.

"Well, then," he said. "When are you leaving?"

"At nine."

He nodded, and I took it to be good-night. I left and went to my own room.

"It was a good movie," I said to Herbert. He looked up

in silence, then returned to what he was doing. He was studying a book called *How to Win Friends and Influence People*, underlining sentences and writing comments in the margin in a large round hand. Besides his interest in Physical Culture, he was fond of books on self-improvement.

In a little while I heard my father's voice giving dictation. Then a clatter of typewriting. He used to work late into the night, preparing his cases for the next day.

XV

One morning, half-way through the term, I was sent for by the headmaster. When I entered he rose to his feet and came around the desk. He said, "I am sorry, I have to tell you that your father has died."

I did not say a word. He said he had known I would take it like a man.

I saw many streets and houses. I was in a thousand rooms; I walked about, and sat, and lay down, and when I looked again I was no longer there. I heard a thousand voices. Some spoke only a word, and others seemed to go on speaking. I had a vision of my life, and there was an unreality about it. I would have to go out and take part in a world that was busy to no purpose. For I could only pretend to be interested.

There had been someone with me up to this point, but from now on I would be alone.

★

The coffin had been placed on the veranda. It was of some

shining metal. Inside it my father lay on his back, dressed in a dark suit. I had never seen him in a dark suit.

Fifty yards away palm trees swayed in the breeze. White-caps were coming to shore, and the motor-boat faced the chop of the waves. I could not believe that I was not in a dream. The coffin would be rolled away, and my father would come down to breakfast, dressed in a white suit as usual. I would hear his car driving away, and in a while I would go swimming, taking a book with me, and lie at the edge of the pool. For these were the summer holidays and there was all the time in the world.

★

We came out of the graveyard, my stepmother being supported by some male relative who had appeared for the occasion. Now that I think of it, Bitsy never seemed to have any relations. We did not know where she came from; she had entered our lives as though she had lighted from another planet. We had known nothing about her family or her past.

As I was going out of the gate a man whom I had seen in my father's office fell in step beside me. His name was Henriques—he was rather boring. Whenever I went to Duke Street he would smile and scrape, eager to please the son of his employer. He would make a joke of the kind that, he thought, would appeal to a schoolboy. He was too familiar.

He said, "I wish to offer my condolences. There are many people who say that Aston Simpson was a hard man. Notwithstanding, I feel that I can state that he was an outstanding member of the legal profession."

He continued in this vein for some moments. His face was soft and wrinkled, as though thousands of small cares had made their way across the surface, day by day, of his smiling affability. Now that his employer was dead he was free to speak, to make a frank estimate of Aston Simpson's qualities. Fearlessly he spoke his mind—and as he spoke he seemed to be aware that, at this time and place, what he had said was rude, that it showed his lack of breeding. And so he persisted, in order to find one sentence, after all, that would justify his bad manners. But the more he spoke the more foolish he sounded. Though my father was not there to hear him, he was still too familiar. He sounded impertinent. He became vindictive. Positively he was hissing. He spoke about an injustice, some matter of a brief that my father had accused him of drawing up wrongly.

"It was not nice to say that in front of the others. Moreover, in all matters of that sort, it was understood that Dennis was to be responsible, not myself. Aston Simpson was very rude on this occasion."

Alfred Henriques was still speaking when I turned away suddenly and went to the car where my brother was waiting. For some reason it had been understood, in making the funeral arrangements, that it would be necessary for my brother and myself to go to the graveyard in one car, and our stepmother in another.

★

We gathered to hear the reading of the will. It was clear and to the point. Herbert was to get a thousand pounds, my father's guns, and the *Encyclopaedia Britannica*. I was given five hundred pounds more—presumably because I was younger and had further to go—and a share in the guns and the *Encyclopaedia*. Aunt Ethel had a hundred pounds. Everything else went to his dear wife, Elizabeth. The house, the law firm, everything. Bitsy was now a rich woman.

My brother and I, said the lawyer, would have to find other accommodations. This was our father's intention. He certainly hadn't intended for Bitsy to support us. Nor was she responsible for my schooling—I would have to pay the fees myself.

When the lawyer had gone, and Aunt Ethel had gone too,

73

saying, "Aston must have taken leave of his senses. To leave everything to that woman!"—my brother told me that we would have to leave the very next day. On this point he was certain—he could not wait to be out of sight of his stepmother.

I did not share Herbert's feelings. I was fond of Bitsy—and I didn't know what Aunt Ethel meant. Fifteen hundred pounds struck me as a fortune. But everyone seemed to be agreed that I had to leave. And Bitsy seemed to think so too. At least, she made no objection.

My brother and I would find a room somewhere. As the furniture as well as the house had been left to Bitsy, the beds in which we had slept since we were children also belonged to her and would have to stay.

So I said goodbye to my half-sister, Bitsy's child, and walked out of the house, carrying my clothes in a suitcase and my books in a box. I would have to come back later to get my bicycle. That was mine, Bitsy admitted—I had paid for it with money I had earned myself. But I would have to fetch it soon. She didn't want it lying around. The same went for the guns and the *Britannica*.

XVI

Jamaicans were struggling for Independence. At night in the streets a crowd would gather and throw stones at the English soldiers. The soldiers fired at the people, and they ran away, leaving two or three lying by the gutters. The next night they were back, to throw more stones.

At the same time a group of Jamaican writers were putting

out a newspaper called *Public Opinion* in which they rallied the people to the cause of Independence. Together with news and editorials there were poems and short stories— written from a Leftist or at least a modern viewpoint.

I came to know these people—among them "Dossie" Carberry and a black poet named Campbell who wrote poems about night, flowers, love—and a young man named Smith who wrote sophisticated prose in which from time to time he used mathematic equations instead of sentences. Smith spoke of authors I had never heard of. In Britain, W. H. Auden and his friends. In America, William Saroyan and Thomas Wolfe. He mentioned a banned book called *Ulysses*—the way he talked about it, *Ulysses* was some sort of black magic.

I tried to read the writers Smith recommended and—with the exception of Wolfe and Saroyan—they struck me as too hard to understand. I admired them all the more. If I could only write like that! Though I couldn't, I tried to write something of my own that would be sophisticated and shocking—that would make people take notice. As I had nothing to say and no story to tell, I wrote confessions: I wrote about the girl I was in love with, in a sort of stream of consciousness—confessing how I felt about her and what I would like to do if I had the opportunity. I titled this "In Love and Puberty", and sent it to *Public Opinion*, thrilled and alarmed by my own daring. The story was published. Aunt Ethel read it and handed it back to me with a sniff. Evidently she thought it disgusting. I had succeeded! *Epater le bourgeois*. I too was now a member of the *avant-garde*. There would be no turning back.

When the English troops were called out and there was shooting in the streets, as I bicycled to meet my friends on *Public Opinion* I felt that I was being involved in a drama of revolution. No one took Jamaica seriously—it was just a place where they grew bananas. But now it had a revolution.

It was making history. You could get killed if you weren't careful.

This thought made me happy; I stayed up late at night, writing poems and stories. It was like being in love . . . and, besides, I *was* in love. At night when I went back to the house where I shared a rented room with my brother, I was ecstatic. I could hardly keep from dancing. The smell of hibiscus and night-jasmine, the stars, the shadows of the Blue Mountains looming by moonlight . . . I couldn't sleep for thinking of the philosophy of Marx—as explained by Smith—and some poems by D. H. Lawrence I had read, and Saroyan's *Daring Young Man on the Flying Trapeze*. All this was mixed up with Gloria's eyes and her figure in a bathing suit.

★

I was filled with impatience to be going about my life, starting my life's work, whatever it might be—I didn't much care. Looking back, I suppose that I intended to be a writer, but I am not at all sure. I think it would be truer to say that a writer was one of the things I intended to be, but that the thought of devoting myself to a profession had not yet become a reality with all its appalling implications. Young men think, when they think about their lives, that they haven't yet begun in earnest. They will get around to writing a masterpiece now and then, when they feel like it and have the time. They will write great novels and poems. But most of the time they will be having romantic adventures. They will run away with beautiful women. They will make speeches in Congress or Parliament. They will be sent to Siberia, and suffer hunger and cold. They will write with a splinter dipped in dye which they have obtained by boiling their shirt. All this without losing their good looks.

But being just a writer? God forbid! Working at it? A dismal prospect. The proper attitude for young men to have in regard to writing was expressed once and for all in the preface to Byron's first book, *Hours of Idleness*, where it says that he "handles his pen with the negligent ease of a gentleman".

But when would I be starting these adventures? In spite of my successes in the *Gleaner* and *Public Opinion*, and the fact that I had an audience—for there must have been others like my aunt who had been alarmed—in spite of being noticed by the world, I was still going to school. I was studying for an exam which, if I did well enough, would send me to Oxford.

I had already passed this exam. Moreover, I had taken it a year earlier than usual. This had put the noses of my enemies out of joint. For I had enemies at school, and they were in Science. When the results of exams came in, and my name was at the top of the list, having got there through literature, history and French, instead of by means of physics and chemistry, these people were visibly disconcerted. They looked at me askance as though I must have cheated; they slinked away and whispered in corners. It had always been the science people who won scholarships to England. Now I had spoiled their plans. And what was I going to make of the success I had, in this surprising, somehow underhanded manner, wrenched out of their grasp? Not much, they wagered. Only poems and stories. They lurked and bided their time. They wished I would fall and break my neck.

Yes, Virginia, there are Two Cultures. But I have never felt sorry that I did not like physics and chemistry. Throughout my boyhood I was compelled to study them—I can't imagine what school it was that C. P. Snow attended, where the readers of poetry, it seems, were not compelled to study chemistry and physics. The moment I could close those infernal books I did so, and have never looked back.

*

It is said of the poet Gray that long after he left Eton he

77

would have dreams in which he was still there—confined and subject to their rules. I too have dreamed that I am still at school. I am sitting in the classroom at night. It is like a lighted box, casting light outward on the barbeque. Other lighted boxes are visible in the dark. These boxes are fed electricity by a dynamo, throbbing on the far side of the barbeque, with now and then a change of sound and an uneasy flickering.

Islands of the night . . . and of the day. For by daylight it is no better. The sun shines every day and time is passing.

The sadness of the tropics is the thought of life vanishing without a mark. You are cut off from the world, and nothing you do will ever be noticed. The indifference of nature is felt more acutely in these out-of-the-way places. "Two things," says Grigoryev, "cry out continually in creation—the sea and man's soul." On an island, the sea is greater than the soul.

Once this was brought home to me when I was with my father. It was Christmas morning; we were in the motor-boat, cruising near the Kingston docks. At one spot a crowd of people were getting into excursion launches. We saw one setting out, packed to the gunwales. My gaze wandered away—to the sky, the peninsula enclosing the harbour, a tanker making its way between the buoys. When I looked at the shore again, the boat of Christmas trippers had vanished. As I gazed, not realizing anything in particular, a moaning sound came from the docks. My father swung the boat in that direction. When we came to the place where the launch had been, only a hat or two floated on the water. The vessel had capsized, carrying forty souls to the bottom with scarcely a splash, and the shining sky was as clear as ever.

I dream that I am still at Hillcastle. Then someone enters, bringing the mail which arrives every night, and he hands me a letter. It tells me that I am to leave for America.

What rushing to pack my suitcase and say good-bye! But then things start to go wrong. I can't find something . . . that I must take with me. I seem to be moving more slowly, and my suitcase hasn't been packed. And the ship is leaving. It has already left. I have missed the connection—and am doomed to stay here for ever, pacing the barbeque, from the main building to the wall—looking down at Alligator Pond and Black River and the empty sea stretching to the horizon.

But this did not happen. When my mother wrote to me I did, indeed, pack in a hurry. Would I like to come to New York for the summer? Indeed, I would. I would have gone anywhere—for all ways led in the same direction, toward my life.

Did I know that I would never be back? I don't think I knew, but unconsciously this may have been what I intended. In any case, a sea voyage and a summer in New York was enough. I did not need to think further than that.

The next day I waited by the road for the mail-van. Every afternoon, just before dusk, it climbed the road to Hillcastle, having come through some forsaken country places. It stopped for a few minutes to drop a mail-bag and take on another. Then it went around the road lined with willows and out the gate. It would go down the mountain to Balaclava, where it connected with the train. And the train would take me, huffing and clanking, with a smell of coal, by way of the cane-fields, and the fields with stacks of logwood, and the slums, to Kingston. From there I would sail for New York.

I put my suitcase on the van and climbed on the front seat beside the driver. The van drove toward the gate. Two boys I knew were sitting on the wall, kicking their heels. They were startled to see me passing. One of them shouted "Where are you going?"

I shouted, "To America!"

79

My father in the night commanding No
Has work to do. Smoke issues from his lips;
    He reads in silence.
The frogs are croaking and the streetlamps glow.

And then my mother winds the gramophone;
The Bride of Lammermoor begins to shriek—
    Or reads a story
About a prince, a castle, and a dragon.

The moon is glittering above the hill.
I stand before the gateposts of the King—
    So runs the story—
Of Thule, at midnight when the mice are still.

And I have been in Thule! It has come true—
The journey and the danger of the world,
    All that there is
To bear and to enjoy, endure and do.

Landscapes, seascapes . . . where have I been led?
The names of cities—Paris, Venice, Rome—
    Held out their arms.
A feathered god, seductive, went ahead.

Here is my house. Under a red rose tree
A child is swinging; another gravely plays.
    They are not surprised
That I am here; they were expecting me.

And yet my father sits and reads in silence,
My mother sheds a tear, the moon is still,
    And the dark wind
Is murmuring that nothing ever happens.

Beyond his jurisdiction as I move
Do I not prove him wrong? And yet, it's true

They will not change
There, on the stage of terror and of love.

The actors in that playhouse always sit
In fixed positions—father, mother, child
    With painted eyes.
How sad it is to be a little puppet!

Their heads are wooden. And you once pretended
To understand them! Shake them as you will,
    They cannot speak.
Do what you will, the comedy is ended.

Father, why did you work? Why did you weep,
Mother? Was the story so important?
    "Listen!" the wind
Said to the children, and they fell asleep.

2

XVII

The first time I saw snow I ate a handful.

Ted Hoffman remembers the incident, and much more besides. Ted was my best friend at Columbia. He too felt out of place. He came from Brooklyn, a long way from the Ivy League.

Recently I wrote Ted asking him to help me rediscover what I felt about Columbia at that time, before the war, and he answered in a long letter that was full of incident and character analysis.

He wrote:

You sought a true education because your childhood prison had postulated it as desirable salvation, but you also succumbed to the injunctions of your parents and elders, without knowing why. "Parents are necessary evils," I do recall discovering and explaining to you once then, and receiving from you great gratitude for my wisdom. Which is to say you feared your mother. You couldn't bear her appearances, her orders . . . she would show up from those Helena Rubinstein trips commanding you to appear at a good restaurant. I must say for all the time I knew you, you had abominable taste in food and liquor, willing to take anything set before you. . . . She would also buy you clothes, usually based on some ridiculous Broadway concept. Why you didn't buy your own clothes I don't know, I guess because you were happy in pants and sweater; I recall watching you dress and pick out any shirt *and any tie*, which even in the depths of Brooklyn was a sign of grossness, which much distressed me when I was counting on your instinctive tastes to define life. I guess you didn't dig money. You didn't seem to know how much you had (*in toto* or at your immediate command) and I'd explain the price of things to you (but values . . . ?). Anyhow it was winter, and you were shivering in the top coat she bought you for fall. I have a mental image of you sweeping a handful of snow off the fender of a car during the first snowfall, licking it and tossing it up in the air, whether out of natural joy or prescribed gesture I can't guess now, and probably didn't consider then. Anyhow, back you came from one of those visits, miserably encased in a big, boxy, nubbly tweed overcoat and a big grey, snap-brim fedora hat (neither Bogart nor Capone, but assuredly the worst of each). I said you looked like a gangster—Louie— and you almost cried, truly in anguish, feeling doomed to walk the campus in that monstrosity because your mother had put it on your head. "Look at it!" you pleaded. "Whatever can I do about it?" "You can take it off right now and throw it in that garbage can," I said. And you did, with great relief, and a Cheshire cat grin. I let you keep the coat, which after all was expensive and warm and you were acclimatized to the Caribbean, and we expected you foreigners to be a little garish.

★

The snow drifted down on my windowsill, forming a sculpture of white grains, millimetre by millimetre. By the end of the day the ledges would be filled with white, sparkling snow, and the street covered with a carpet, inches deep.

Children would be out, sledding down snowbanks with loud cries. I knew them by their boots, earmuffs and mittens. They were figures out of the Montgomery Ward catalogue I had looked at years ago on a veranda. They were part of the American landscape. Some day I too would have merged with the landscape, if I could stand the cold.

XVIII

On Fridays I used to go to Brooklyn. I went on the subway, watching the stations—Franklin, Nostrand, Kingston—and emerging at dusk on an avenue walled with apartment houses. There were men with black hats, side-curls and beards, and old women sitting on benches along the parkway, facing the street. The headlights swept shadows of heads and shoulders across the walls.

I entered one of the apartment houses and went through a lobby that was dimly lit like a corridor in a ship. I went up in the elevator, which smelled of cooking, and pushed a doorbell. The door was opened by a tall, stout woman—my grandmother. She embraced me and kissed me on the head.

"Dollink!"

She was Jewish—and I was a Jew. I had not known this before I met her. I had known that my mother's family came from Russia, but not that they were Jews. In fact when I was gowing up I hardly knew that Jews existed. I only saw them mentioned in books, as people who spoke with a thick accent and lent money at a high rate of interest.

And now I had discovered that I was a Jew. But I didn't feel Jewish.

Not that I felt like a Christian, either. At school I had been compelled to go to chapel twice a day, every day, with an extra-long session on Sunday. As a punishment I had been compelled to memorize psalms and recite them aloud. There is nothing like a religious upbringing for making you bored with religion for the rest of your life. Moreover, I hadn't noticed that Christianity made people tolerant and kind. I did not think that I would lose much by not being a Christian.

But to be a Jew! What did I know about Judaism? I didn't like what I had seen of the Jews on New Lots Avenue. The side-curls! The religious complexion, like the belly of a dead fish. . . . And the language they spoke! If turnips and cabbages had a voice, they would speak Yiddish.

In any case, I was not religious. And if you weren't a religious Jew, what kind of Jew were you?

But this was not the question—religion had nothing to do with it. It was race that counted. You were a Jew because you had "Jewish blood". People in Europe were finding this out. There were people in Germany of the better class— who had been to a university, with the duelling scars to prove it, who could quote Schiller and Goethe, and wouldn't have deigned to spit on a Russian Jew. . . . Suddenly these people had been informed that they had "Jewish blood". They were not Germans, they were Jews—in the same herring-barrel with Litvaks and Russian Jews.

According to the racists I was a Jew. A clear case—for my mother was Jewish. But I didn't feel like a Jew. As far as my feelings went, I might as well have been told I was an Indian.

Maybe this was how the Indians felt. Till the white man came they had not known they were Indians. They were people, and did not know that there were any other kind. Then, suddenly, they were told that they were Indians.

You were an Indian, or a Jew, because other people thought you were.

★

The family met at my grandmother's on Friday—everyone but my mother; she was in Caracas, selling cosmetics to the Venezuelans. My aunt Ruth came from her job at the front desk of Charles-of-the-Ritz; Cousin Dorothy from

Wall Street, where she worked for a stockbroker; Uncle Joe from Times Square—he was a pharmacist and worked in Whelan's drugstore; Aunt Annette from an employment agency for actors and song-and-dance people. One by one they arrived, hung up their coats and umbrellas, and offered to help in the kitchen, but my grandmother told them to sit down. They must be tired from working.

She lit the candles and prayed, and carried the prayer with a sweeping motion into her heart. Then she served the meal—chicken soup, radishes and celery, boiled meat, chicken, carrots and peas. While they ate, her children talked about the events of the week—what a customer said, the opening of a new show on Broadway.

She turned her face to the one who was speaking. Everything they said seemed to strike her as a wonder. She had lived thirty years in America and it was still all wonderful to her.

She wept for her people in Russia, and trusted in God and Franklin Delano Roosevelt.

XIX

The instructor's hands were thin and the green veins stood out. The index and third finger were stained with nicotine.

He had been talking for some time, explaining Ricardo's theory of value, and I was not following what he was saying. I was listening to the sound of his voice rather than what he actually said, noticing his hands which moved about as he talked. Now and then he would jump up from the chair and write on the blackboard. Sometimes he sat on the edge of the table. He lit another cigarette. Then, in the middle of a sentence, he began to cough. His chest heaved and he snatched a handkerchief out of his pocket and coughed into it. He sounded as though he had consumption.

This man had written books that had been translated into several languages. He was teaching a course called Contemporary Civilization. But it seemed from the nicotine stains on his fingers and the way he coughed that what he liked best was smoking.

When he had finished coughing it seemed that he sensed what we were thinking, for he strode to and fro, glaring first at one, then at another, and speaking more vehemently. Then he settled on the edge of the table again and crossed his legs and clasped his right knee in his hands. Hands which for forty years had crawled over sheets of paper, writing so many books. The man himself had been only the attachment to a hand that wrote and wrote. A hand that got up in the morning to write.

After these classes I could hardly remember what had been said. The instructor had uttered a great number of words on a subject he knew well, but it is necessary to experience something for oneself in order to know it. The instructor dealt in abstractions. He provided the student with quantities of words which signified a number of things. If the student remained for a long time in the university he would be encapsulated in words, like the instructor, and there would come a day when he would not have to deal with anything but the shell of words surrounding him. He would touch the smooth walls on every side and think this was reality.

*

Besides Contemporary Civilization, I was required to take a course called the Humanities. This consisted of reading and discussing great books from Herodotus to Dostoievsky. Our instructor was Lionel Trilling. He had hazel eyes and a charming smile. He conducted the discussions gracefully and always seemed to have something more to say than he actually revealed. The object of our reading seemed to be to find ideas we could argue about. Ideas were what we were after, not feelings or a sense of the way the work was written. We were certainly not reading for pleasure. I kept finding things that pleased me, however, and Trilling corrected me every time. My pleasure in the work itself was not to the point. He brought the discussion back to the idea we were pursuing. It seemed that we were about to find it when the bell rang and our instructor vanished. On Monday next it would be another book and another great idea.

I was also taking a course in English literature, with Raymond Weaver. Weaver would make a dramatic entrance, then sit at his desk without saying a word for a minute or so. Then, glaring at a student and in a deep, resonant voice, he would launch a question. The questions were intended to mystify. Once when he did this—"What is Aristotle's *Poetics* about?"—I answered immediately, "How to write a play." As this spoiled the suspense he was aiming at, he pretended not to have heard.

Weaver wore dove colours; he was an aesthete, and would have been at home in the 'nineties. As is common with such people, he was suspicious of those who, like himself, were aesthetes; he favoured the unimaginative, athletic types. He had a trick that underlined this prejudice. He would recite "Casey at the Bat".

Ten thousand eyes were on him as he rubbed his hands with dirt,
Five thousand tongues applauded when he wiped them on his shirt;

Then while the writhing pitcher ground the ball into
   his hip,
Defiance gleamed in Casey's eye, a sneer curled Casey's
   lip.

Then he would recite Dowson's poem about Cynara.

I cried for madder music and for stronger wine,
But when the feast is finished and the lamps expire,
Then falls thy shadow, Cynara! the night is thine;
And I am desolate and sick of an old passion,
   Yea hungry for the lips of my desire:
I have been faithful to thee, Cynara! in my fashion.

Then he would ask which was poetry. Inevitably some poor
fish would bite, saying that "Cynara" was poetry and
"Casey" wasn't. Whereupon, in his booming voice,
Weaver would explain the pretentiousness of "Cynara", its
insincerity, its essential vulgarity.

*

I would meet Ted for lunch at the New Asia. My freshman year at Columbia had a distinct flavour of soy sauce.
The history of the Peloponnesian War came with an egg
roll and fried rice, and the cogitations of Ricardo were
mixed with Chinese vegetables. Now that I think about it,
these surroundings were suitable, for the liberal arts at
Columbia were served simultaneously in little portions, like
dishes in a Chinese restaurant—a mouthful of St. Augustine,
a spoonful of Spinoza, a small helping of Huxley. The
object, I suppose, was to make you hungry later.
   Ted and I discussed current events. I said, with my mouth
full of noodles, "Poor little Finland! I don't give a damn
about Finland, what's important is the Russian army. Let's
face it, they are the ones who are going to have to fight
the Nazis. At least we know now that their artillery is
good."

I was one of the leading authorities on Marxism among College freshmen. Also, as I had been in a revolution in the Caribbean and had seen the workers shot down in cold blood—this was the impression my friends had gathered, and I did not try to correct it—I was the leading authority on street fighting and military strategy and tactics. I was ruthless in my attitude toward the Finns. Individuals and small nations didn't matter. Only the future mattered.

Sometimes we were joined for lunch by Bob Shafner. He had an easy, superior manner. Bob was very much the New Yorker. He had gone to Horace Mann high school and was now getting A's in Columbia Colllege. There were dozens of Bobs at Columbia; they seemed to have learned all the answers long ago. They ran campus activities and were going into journalism, law, or medicine. Already in his freshman year Bob was taking professional courses.

A few years after graduating he would be established in his profession. He would have married a good-looking girl. They would have an apartment on Park Avenue and rent a house in the Hamptons every summer. Bob would take up sail-boating. Their living-room would be decorated with paintings by Larry Rivers, and Norman Mailer would come to one of their parties. If Mailer couldn't make it, Gore Vidal.

But I am anticipating. We are still in the New Asia restaurant. Ted, in the plaid sports jacket, is exchanging Joycean puns with Bob Shafner, who is more suitably dressed for the Ivy League, in grey flannel. The author of *Ulysses* is one of their heroes—Groucho Marx is another.

The third man, myself—we have already seen how he dresses—is trying to get a word in edgewise. When he does, it will be some enthusiastic outburst; it will probably be off the point, and it will probably be about Marcel Proust, whom he has been reading again. They will listen to him tolerantly, then Ted will say something to modify the out-

93

burst and make it more acceptable, or Bob Shafner will dispose of it with a witty remark. But tolerantly, for Shafner is a well-rounded man, and this is his day for seeing his literary friends. Back at the fraternity when they twit him with it, he says, "It takes all kinds."

"This talk of war . . . " Bob said, "you don't know what real trouble is. I have to go see Sammy Kaye's agent this afternoon and persuade him to let Sammy play for us."

Ted and I looked at him in silence. The man of affairs.

"The prom is only a few months away," he explained.

Not only did Bob have to get a band for the prom, but also he had to see Dean Hawkes that afternoon and plead the case of a fraternity brother who had got into trouble and was on the verge of being expelled from the college.

"What kind of trouble?"

He put his finger to his lips. A man of important secrets.

"And tonight I'm taking Betty to see *Pal Joey*. I had a helluva time getting tickets. They charge an arm and a leg. But I had to . . . she's been after me. Women are expensive, let me tell you."

A man of the world.

When Bob left to see the Dean, Ted and I were subdued. I had a class in French that afternoon, but after listening to Bob's real-life activities, I wondered if it was worth studying French. Those long drifting sentences of *La Recherche du Temps Perdu*. . . . What was it someone had said about Proust and his interminable explorations of the psyche? Proust was like a man in a bathtub, wallowing in his own dirty bath water.

I had once met Bob with his Betty—or was it another girl? He dated several. This was a pretty brunette, with a sparkling, humorous face. She shook hands with me, interested to be introduced to "my friend the poet", but I couldn't think of anything to say. She looked at me and waited, but I couldn't think of anything.

94

Bob said, "Well now, keep at it," and they walked off. I saw him handing her into a taxi.

I consoled myself with thinking that she would be unfaithful to him. All women were unfaithful, and love was a disease. I knew that from my reading in Proust.

XX

I was tutoring two children. When they had done their homework I would take them to Riverside Drive with their dog.

It was so that I met Bonnie. She watched me throwing a ball, and the dog and Hans and his sister Amelie scampering after it. One or the other of them would return panting with the ball, and I'd throw it again.

Once the dog brought the ball back to Bonnie, and so she joined in the ball-throwing. Her legs were too fat, but she had a lovely face, bright eyes, black hair. It was a pity about her legs, but this one defect made it possible for me to talk to her. If she had been perfect I would have been speechless.

Every afternoon she happened to be there, on the walk near the Soldiers' and Sailors' Monument. Little Hans grew sulky because I would be rapt in conversation with Bonnie and no longer willing to discuss the American Civil War and the Far West and other matters that his parents, having escaped from Germany, wanted him to be familiar with, in order to be Americanized. While I talked to Bonnie, Sister Amelie looked downright jealous behind her thick glasses.

Bonnie was in high school and was impressed with everything I said about college life. At this time I had discovered a teacher I liked—Mark Van Doren. I was in the seminar he gave in the poems of Thomas Hardy and W. B. Yeats. I aired my ideas about poetry on the Drive, with Bonnie for an audience.

It occurred to me that I could see her when I was not with the children. I asked her to come up to Columbia and look around, and she said yes as though there were nothing unusual about the request. I was to pick her up at her apartment.

The person who opened the door wasn't the girl of the Soldiers' and Sailors' Monument, with red mittens and earmuffs. This one was dressed like an Easter rabbit, in pink, with ribbons and bows. When I took her on the trolley up to Columbia, and when I walked her around the campus, everyone stared. I passed two or three people I knew—I nodded stiffly and they looked surprised. I caught them looking back at us.

Bonnie was gay. She wanted to know who the bronze lady was, holding up one of her hands with the palm open.

"Alma Mater," I said.

"She looks as if she's saying, Don't blame me."

I took her down to the Lion's Den. This was where the College men brought their girls. Bob Shafner came over to our table. "Mind if we join you?" he said. He was with a girl with red hair. I said not at all, and soon we were all talking. Bob kept deferring to me for my opinion on this and that—I had never seen him so deferential. Bonnie rolled her eyes and made little mouths of approval or disapproval. Now and then she would be convulsed with laughter and have to wipe a tear from the corner of an eye.

The redhead wasn't so talkative. She kept looking at her watch. Then she got up suddenly and left. Bob got up too and hurried after her. They spoke together briefly, then he returned to the table, shrugging his shoulders.

When we left the Lion's Den, Bob walked us over to Broadway. He waved a cheery goodbye.

"Take care of him, Bonnie," he said. "Mind now! He's a wonderful guy."

★

I wasn't in love with Bonnie. I just had a feeling of excitement when I went to the Drive, and a sinking feeling if she were late, and a feeling of relief when she appeared. But she was too flamboyant for my taste, and the two or three times I took her out—to Columbia, to the movies—I was actually embarrassed to be seen with her. And her bell-like laugh . . . I wished she wouldn't laugh like that, so that people turned around.

She thought I was a scream. Once when we were looking at a parade, and a platoon came marching by in the costume of the old British redcoats, with high bearskin hats, I said, "I thought we won that war." Bonnie went off in a peal of laughter and the redcoats nudged each other in the ribs.

Once when I picked her up to take her to the movies she had put on a new dress and looked so beautiful that I said, "What's this? Hallowe'en?" And Bonnie went off in a scream.

★

I hadn't ever kissed her. I did hold her hand, however, crossing streets, and I wrote a few poems in which love was mentioned in a rather cynical manner. Sometimes it was the cynicism of Hardy in his *Satires of Circumstance*—a woman burying her husband and going off with a lover. At times the cynicism was French, in the manner of Laforgue—the gentleman visitor thinks that the lady has become a little stale.

It was always assumed that, for one reason or another, love was an illusion. Either the lover was betrayed or the loved one died.

Life imitates art. Or is it simply that art mirrors the tendencies which determine life? One day I was coming back to the dormitory in the dusk, from the library where I had been reading. It was drizzling. It had been one of those days that seemed to express the monotony of a scholar's life—in which any page you turned was like the rain outside, dismal and repetitious.

I heard a peal of laughter. Then two figures went past me in the rain—a man and a girl. She was sheltering under his raincoat. It was Bonnie, and the man was Bob Shafner. They didn't see me—they were too engrossed in each other.

I went up to my room and paced to and fro. I was unable to sit down for more than a few seconds. I lay down on the bed and immediately stood up again. I tried reading, but it was no use. I was filled with bitterness and rage. Then . . . a calm resolve—I would never speak to her again.

When next she appeared on Riverside Drive, coming toward me with a light in her eyes—I said, "I don't want to see you again." I turned away, with little Hans and Amelie and the dog, and left her standing there.

XXI

One January morning I left my steam-heated room at Columbia and took the subway down to the Armory, a black building with castellated walls on Fourth Avenue.

There I joined a line of draftees. We were loaded on trucks and transported to Fort Dix, New Jersey. We removed our clothing and stood in line. The line moved forward; supply sergeants thrust olive-drab clothing, eating utensils and gas-masks at us, and we emerged at the end of the line as soldiers.

For a few days we sluiced the barracks floors and "policed the area", picking up bits of fluff from the gravel between the buildings. Then we were divided in groups, marched to the railhead, and sent off in boxcars. All day the train clickety-clacked, hooting across a wilderness with shacks straggling away from the rails. At night when the stopping train jerked me awake I looked out on the stilly lights of strange cities.

My destination was a tank regiment in Texas. On the first evening in camp, for want of anything else to do, I sat in the room where men were writing letters home—how intently they bent their heads and wrote!—and looked at the tank-training manuals. There were diagrams of tank tactics, trajectories of fire, etc. It didn't look like much of a future. A bugle sounded us to bed.

Before dawn I woke, shivering with cold. I had never been so cold in my life. While it was still dark the bugle sounded reveille. Though we had worn our long-johns to bed—a garment of grey-white woollen underwear—getting out was like getting into a cold bath. The naked moment of putting your feet on the floor! Someone threw lumps of coal into the iron stove and lit it. We dressed as close to the heat as we could, then fell out under the frosty stars, and were shoved and commanded by the sergeants into the semblance of a company formation.

Before dawn the tanks loomed as shadows against the sky, with high turrets and cannons like elephants' trunks. When morning filtered through the bleak sky the shadows parted revealing machines of a remarkable ugliness, lopsided metal

99

boxes studded with rivets. These were the General Grants, created on a design exactly opposite to that which was needed in tanks. In a tank you want a low silhouette and a long gun; the Grant had a short gun and a high silhouette. But I was not concerned with field problems. What troubled me was the machinery—for example, the track, a belt of iron teeth which, our sergeant informed us, would sometimes break; we would then have to kink it together again, as though it were a watch-strap. My fingers, crammed into my pockets where I was trying to warm them, were anticipating being flattened between the sledgehammer and teeth of broken track. We climbed into the turret. The gun breeches, with a cold rap now and then, promised to knock our brains out. Here, the sergeant explained, shells would be stacked all around us. I could see myself being blown to smithereens, or, more likely, fried to a crisp. I have met infantrymen who wanted to be in the Air Force; for my part, I yearned for a transfer to a mere rifle company.

We were given instruction in tank driving. The idea was simple. You pulled on a lever that braked one track; the other track would keep going and the tank would lurch in the braked direction. The farm boys, fresh from their tractors, had no trouble with this, neither did truck drivers from Brooklyn, but I had never driven anything but a bicycle. At one point my instructor shouted, "Jesus Christ!" and swung at my head with a monkey wrench—though I don't believe he was really trying to kill me; it was just self-defence. They listed me not as a driver, but as loader and radioman.

Meanwhile we were learning to roll a pack and march; to take apart, put together, and shoot a tommy gun, rifle, pistol, and .30 calibre machine-gun. Also we did KP, the bane of enlisted men, which calls you out of bed in the freezing dark to go and serve the cook—and all cooks are ill-tempered—clearing away swill, and scouring greasy pots, and peeling potatoes, until—when it seems you will never escape—you have scrubbed down the last table and are released to grope your way back to bed by starlight. During this period, also, we were trotted, in our heavy overcoats, from the drill field to heated rooms where we were shown movies. I remember one about the consequences of fornication. Who was the fine actor with half a face who made such an impression on the theatre-goers of Camp Bowie? He was more appalling than the Phantom of the Opera as he told in a mournful voice how he had got that way.

The aim of military training is not just to prepare men for battle, but to make them long for it. Inspections are one way to achieve this. When you've washed the barracks windows and floor till they are speckless, you arrange your clothing and equipment in symmetrical patterns on and around a bed made tight as a drum. You stand at attention while a colonel and your company officers pass by. Sometimes the colonel stops in front of you. He may ask you to recite one of the sacred orders of guard duty; he may look through the barrel of your weapon, or harass you in a new way.

The colonel stopped in front of me. "Soldier", he said, "do you believe in God?" For weeks no one had asked my opinion about anything. My vanity was roused and I seized the opportunity to star. I hesitated, then said, "No, sir."

In a moment the air seemed to have become as fragile as glass. I had already begun to be sorry. The colonel spoke again, "Solider, look out of that window."

I looked. There was a brown glimpse of Texas and a slice of sky. There were the tanks drawn up in rows.

"Who made all that?"

Someone else might have replied, "General Motors," but I didn't. Retreating from my exposed position as fast as possible, I said, "I suppose it was God, sir."

The colonel told me that He had, and not to forget it, and proceeded on his way.

When the officers had left the barracks, my platoon sergeant stared at me and exclaimed bitterly, "Why did he have to ask *him*!"

The sergeant was a Regular Army man. The war, which I thought of as a personal experience which was adding to my education, was just another job to him, and the only important thing was to do it right. Of such is the Kingdom of Heaven.

*

The regiment was sent to Hood. Today, in city apartments, housing developments, offices and gas stations and supermarkets, there are hundreds of thousands of men joined by one silent name—Hood! Conceive a plain of absolute brown, broken only by clumps of thorn and stunted trees, and, in the middle of this desert, white barracks laid out in perfect rectangles; a city in the middle of nowhere, housing eighty thousand souls. The sun rises and stirs this ant heap; men march here and there; they enter machines and the machines proceed in files into the desert where, in clouds of dust, they dart to and fro or stand immobile. At noon the plain is burning with heat. Then the machines return to the centre; the ant files wind back to their nests. Stars swim out and the plain is gripped with cold.

Hood was for the training of tank destroyers and a handful of tanks. The tank destroyers were open armoured cars with wheels in front and tracks in the rear, mounting a cannon. They were supposed to knock out tanks with one or two well-placed projectiles and depart at speed before they could be hit. That, at least, was the theory. Our tanks were supposed to manoeuvre with or against them.

We turned out in the freezing dawn. I climbed into the tank turret, put on my helmet, and strapped myself to the seat. The tank lurched with whining engines and jingling, squeaking tracks over the plain. When the sun rose, through the periscope I glimpsed jigsaw pieces of sky and earth. We travelled in clouds of dust. Dust entered by every crack; it turned our green fatigues brown and filled our nostrils. Through the earphones, which as radioman I wore, came sounds of command, drawling Tennessee and nervous New Jersey, exchanged by the lieutenants and sergeants. At noon we panted in universal heat. At the end of the day we joggled home and came to a stop. But the task was not over. The tank guns then had to be cleaned and greased—the seventy-five by pushing a ramrod down its snout—and sometimes a track had to be repaired. While the infantryman returned to barracks, cleaned his rifle, showered, and went his way to chow and a movie, we struggled with our monster, cursing, shoving, sledgehammering.

Hood! It was there we beat the Germans. There, shivering at dawn and sweating at noon, we endured the climate of Africa and pestilent Kwajalein. The iron of which those tanks were made entered our souls. Hood was our university. There we got our real education, which set us off from the men who came before and the men who came after. Sometimes in speaking to older men I have sensed there is a veil between us; and to a man of twenty-five there are things I cannot explain.

Under certain conditions human nature can be changed into something else. A man can be changed from a political animal into a machine—articulated to climb or leap from a height, to swing a sledgehammer, to dig with a shovel. His instincts can be trained so that with fingers from which all doubt has departed he can pick apart a machine gun under a blanket and assemble it again. Turn men out of their offices, separate them from the flesh of women, and books, and chairs; expose them to the naked sky and set them drudging at physical tasks, and in a few months you can change the mind itself. Religion, philosophy, mathematics, art, and all the other abstractions, can be blotted out as though they never existed. This is how Ur and Karnak vanished and this is how the Ice Age will return.

For recreation in the evenings I'd take the bus—you couldn't walk the distances—to the main PX, and fill myself with beer and ice-cream, and smoke a cigar. Or go to the movies. At that time Holywood was producing patriotic musical comedies; in the finale, soldiers, sailors, marines and chorus girls marked time with a hand salute while Old Glory spread fluttering on the screen.

On our rare two-day passes we went on desperate expeditions. The nearest settlement, Killeen, was not a town but a street trodden into mud by boot soles, like a cattle wallow. There were no women in Killeen. So we swarmed to towns hundreds of miles away—Fort Worth, or sparkling new, sky-scrapered Dallas, or Houston—there, after prowling the streets and parks, once more to enter a theatre and gaze at pictures. The aroma of popcorn . . . the slumped shoulders of the soldier snoring in the seat before you . . . then the propulsion once more into the streets, the glare of afternoon, with nothing to do but eat in a greasy restaurant and return to camp. . . .

Most accounts of army life describe a variety of characters, but I do not remember any who were remarkable. My tank crew included a soft-spoken Southern sergeant; a driver with a rugged build and a face like a boot; and a half-witted fellow named Maniscalco. When I went to town, it was usually with a fat boy from New York named Marvin and a Jersey boy named Bob. Marvin sprinkled his conversation with French words got out of books. We made a rakish threesome in the streets, threatening the virtue of stenographers, but nothing came of it.

All at once, by a stroke of good fortune, Marvin, Bob and I were taken out of the tanks. The army had instituted a programme of specialized training in order to turn enlisted men into technicians. I applied for language training. When the orders came we were all listed for engineering. I did not quibble; I packed my bags and left.

There is an epilogue to this history of the tanks. Years later in Manhattan, travelling on the subway, I saw the face of Maniscalco, the half-wit of my crew. I asked him what had happened to the company after I left.

"We went overseas," he said. "You was lucky to get out. The tank was hit by a shell. We was all wounded and the driver was killed."

★

The specialized training programme was a fraction of the sum of waste, the incalculable extravagance of war. Bob, Marvin and I were sent to Louisiana State University and housed among lawns and flowering shrubs. In the morning we marched to classes, and for an hour in the afternoon we did calisthenics. It must have rapidly become clear that most of the trainees were not qualified to be engineers, yet the programme continued while, around half the world, slender battalions, gasping for relief, bore the brunt of the fighting.

We knew how lucky we were and had no qualms about it. In our spare time we loafed around the swimming pool. This easy life, together with heavy Army meals, began to make us puffy. Marvin discovered that some of the Louisiana girls spoke a kind of French; his line of French patter struck them as hilarious, and in no time at all we had dates. In the evenings, on the banks of the Mississippi, I found myself wrestling with a young woman who smelled like a cosmetics counter. These conflicts left me weak, and it was as much as I could do to get out of bed at reveille.

But, for all I know, Louisiana belles may still be as chaste as Diana, for the training programme was scrapped as suddenly as it started, and I was sent off to an infantry division in Missouri. Bob and Marvin were shipped to an armoured division; I congratulated myself on having the better luck.

It was the middle of winter. Somehow I got delayed in transit, and when I wandered into the headquarters of my new division, at Fort Leonard Wood, on a freezing December night, I was received with anything but joy.

"Your outfit is out there," said a first sergeant, pointing into the black Missouri woods and hills. "Find it."

Lugging my pack and rifle I wandered through the night. It was snowing fitfully; here and there campfires burned. Inquiring the way, at last I arrived at the right company, the right platoon, and the right squad, huddled round a fire in their blankets, with their boots practically in the embers. The squad corporal, a wiry young Italian, seemed possessed by devils. Uttering a stream of obscenity he showed me a machine-gun mounted on a tripod.

"You're the ammo bearer," he said. "Stand guard over that gun. What are you, one of those fuggin ASTP jerks? Doan give me any of your fuggin crap!"

I stood over the gun in the cutting wind, with snow driving into my face. The bleak day rose. Men stirred, groaned, and got to their feet. They dragged dry branches to the fire and heated their rations in blackened mess kits. They were like a company of the dead. I had been assigned, it seemed, to the worst fuggin company, of the worst fuggin division, in the army.

Experience confirmed this impression. The outfit was a kind of factory for turning out infantry replacements who would go overseas. The division itself never hoped to move. On the muddy, snow-covered hills of Missouri it stumbled to and fro, cursing obscenely. The air had a smell of coal smoke and rusty iron. I stepped along in the files of the damned, carrying ammunition boxes that grew heavy as lead. And behind me, or in front, or to one side, howled the infernal corporal, Fugg.

One day I found my name on the bulletin board; I was to gather my equipment and present myself at company headquarters. There the captain made a speech disclaiming all responsibility for our incapacity, saluted with a final downward motion of the arm as though consigning us to hell, and released us from his jurisdiction. We were marched on to a train, and a few days later reached the Atlantic. Carrying our heavy barracks bags over one shoulder we filed up a ramp on to the deck of a ship and groped our way down ladders into the hold. So at last I went to war.

"Military servitude"—Vigny's phrase—how well it describes life in barracks! Details, drill, inspections, field problems, parades—the way of life of Regular Army men—all this was intolerable.

Action was better. In training you were always anticipating combat; you were oppressed by many anxieties. In action you confronted the worst and could hope for an end of things.

★

Who is the soldier with my face? He is strangely galvanized.

Holland . . . the churchyard at Veghel. . . . We have turned off the road into a churchyard. It seems we are to dig in here between the gravestones. Not at all conscious of the irony—irony and other defence mechanisms fade under pressure—we begin our excavations. I am about a foot down when an airburst cracks over our heads and fragments of metal hum by, thwack against tree trunks, slice into the ground.

In a wink the company has vanished. We are lying on our faces in a hot passion of burrowing.

More airbursts follow, one after the other. It's a trap and we're caught in it. The Germans must have eighty-eights looking right down our throats.

Someone is shouting, "Medic!"

There's a tap on my left shoulder-blade and something trickles down my back. Blood. I've been hit.

I hear my name being called. It's the sergeant. I crawl out of my hole and approach him on knees and elbows, cradling my rifle in my arms.

"Go back to Headquarters Section. Tell them the mortars are out of ammunition."

I get to my feet and run crouching between the graves. I'm aware of explosions all around and a humming of jagging iron. But I have a strange feeling of joy. I've been tagged already—I'm safe. But, more than this, I'm exhilarated at the prospect of doing something.

I get to Headquarters and find the sergeant kneeling over clover-leaf containers of mortar shells.

"Take these up," he says.

A container under each arm, rifle slung over a shoulder, I begin the journey. More airbursts. Bullets are flying too, but I don't hear them.

I get to the mortars and let the containers down into the hands of the crew. They look grateful. I start back for more.

And now I've lost count of the trips. As I run I feel like a broken-field runner on his lucky day.

ARM IN ARM

Arm in arm in the Dutch dyke
Were piled both friend and foe
With rifle, helmet, motor-bike:
Step over as you go.

They laid the Captain on a bed
Of gravel and green grass.

The little Dutch girl held his head
And motioned us to pass.

Her busy hands seemed smooth as silk
To a soldier in the sun,
When she gave him a jug of milk
In which his blood did run.

O, had the Captain been around
When trenching was begun,
His bright binoculars had found
The enemy's masked gun!

Beside a Church we dug our holes,
By tombstone and by cross.
They were too shallow for our souls
When the ground began to toss.

Which were the new, which the old dead
It was a sight to ask.
One private found a polished head
And took the skull to task

For spying on us . . . Till along
Driving the clouds like sheep,
Our bombers came in a great throng,
And so we fell asleep.

XXII

To remember a battle in which he has taken part, a man
must make himself innocent again—innocent of newspapers,

books and movies. He must remember his actual life, the life of the body. Everything else is journalism.

I was lying on a ridge from which I could see the plain surrounding Rheims. A wind was driving the clouds before it and cloud shadows flitted over the plain. I could see the tents of the 101st Airborne Division, to which I belonged, laid out in rows.

The 101st and the 82nd Airborne had fought in Normandy, leading the invasion. In September we were used again, dropping in Holland in an attempt to turn the German line at Arnheim. The attempt had failed, and the fighting petered out in drizzle and mud. Then we were withdrawn to rest areas.

I was lying in what appeared to be a trench—a ditch, nearly filled in, with scraps of rusty wire here and there, winding along the ridge. It must have been dug by soldiers of the First World War. I was thinking this over and smoking my pipe. In the distance was Rheims, with the cathedral sailing through the clouds.

My thoughts were interrupted. Among the tents there was a flurry of walking figures. Trucks were arriving, and men jumping down from the tail-gates. Some of them were reeling. They looked like men who had been dragged out of bars in a hurry. I went down to join them, making for my tent in Headquarters Section of one of the glider-infantry companies.

When I entered, the First Sergeant shouted, "Full field in fifteen minutes! O.D.'s and sweater." In fifteen minutes we would have to be dressed and ready for combat. But perhaps it was only an inspection. I stripped to my long-johns and dressed again as ordered. I got into my paratroop boots. When I had on my overcoat, I festooned myself with equipment, gas-mask, pack, belt with articles attached to it—canteen, trench-tool, bayonet. I tied the combat knife to my right leg. I put my helmet-liner into its steel shell. I grabbed my rifle from the rack and a cleaning rod, and passed two patches through the barrel. Then the non-coms began handing out boxes of K-rations, clips of bullets, bandoliers of bullets, and hand-grenades. Apparently it was not going to be an inspection. I slung bandoliers over my shoulders and filled my pockets with rations and grenades.

Whistles blew. We piled out of the tents and formed squads and platoons. Our captain appeared, facing us. The non-coms called our names and we answered "Yo!" The First Sergeant swivelled and shouted at the Captain, "All present and accounted for, sir!" Under our bear-like overcoats we sweated. It had been a lively fifteen minutes.

A line of open "cattle trucks" drew up abreast of the company. We were marched off in platoons. We lifted ourselves and our equipment into the trucks. Colliding at close quarters, we muttered the usual obscenities. We were packed in, side by side. There was no conversation. The trucks began to move.

The convoy wound through a grey landscape. I dozed off, but the truck would jolt to a stop, jerking me awake. There was a shifting of somnolent men. The truck moved again. We passed through villages with narrow streets, houses of stone with shuttered windows. A chilly wind pried down your back and your feet were numb. Hours passed. When it grew dark the trucks turned on their lights. Once the convoy stopped to unload for five minutes. At the roadside where I was awkwardly fumbling with my buttons, a few citizens—an old woman, a middle-aged man, a child—stood watching us. They too were laconic. We clambered back into the trucks.

If an infantryman had his way, he would sleep out the war. But he is shaken back to life and the fear of death.

What is terrible is not the day you have screwed up your nerve to meet. It is the day after that, when you are compelled to go into danger again. At such moments courage is cold. Yet the shells and bullets are no less real than they were yesterday. Then it is that the heart is gripped by fear, and as you smoke a cigarette and stare at an object, or a face, or a patch of light, the lines are inscribed in your mind forever.

The night was dark; there was a rumbling of guns. The convoy stopped moving.

"Dismount!"

We climbed out and formed ranks. Someone dropped his helmet on the road with a fearful clang. We were marched off at combat interval—in two files, staggered, with the men several paces apart.

The company struck off the road, marching over sloping ground. We were in a forest of black trees. All at once the files jerked forward and extended and you practically had to run to keep up. The files stopped again, and you waited. Under your clothing sweat trickled; then it became cold and clammy.

A whisper came down the line: "Fall out!"

I sat down and leaned against my pack. We rested there for five minutes.

"On your feet!" The chase started again. We were pursuing idiotic captains and lieutenants through the woods.

Again the company telescoped. "This is it. Dig in!"

We were facing downhill. I unslung my equipment, propped the rifle against the pack, and took the trench-tool out of its carrier. I turned the blade at an angle to the haft and clamped it, for digging. When you've been sitting in a truck for hours, and running through the night, it's a relief to do something with your hands. You mark a rectangle in the ground, grave-size; then you hack out the dirt. In a few minutes when I looked around the men near me had sunk to their knees. We were sinking at the same rate.

As I dug something wet struck my cheek. Again! It was

starting to snow. Flakes came drifting down. In a little while the earth was glimmering white and the chipping of trench-tools was muted.

We finished our holes at about the same time. They were yards apart and there was no reason for us to speak. I broke a branch, heavy with cones, from a fir tree, and dragged it over my hole. I put my pack and rifle in the bottom of the hole, and laid out my sleeping bag. The human body is standard; there's a time when all the soldiers lie down as one man.

The First Sergeant appeared. He said, "Pack up! We're moving."

The insults of army life make you almost willing to fight. Cursing our officers we marched for another half-hour. When we got to the place we were to hold, it was just another hillside. Had someone made a mistake? Or changed his mind? These were things I never knew. But if I had known, it wouldn't have made any difference. I would still have had to dig a foxhole.

★

"You're on guard," said a shadow leaning above me. I climbed out of my hole and looked around. Close by, the snow-laden boughs were glimmering. Beyond, in a semi-circle, the night was spotted with fires. The clouds over there were flame-coloured. I heard a rumbling of cannon and rattling of machine-guns. Yet here everything was still.

At dawn, fog clung to the earth and was suspended in wisps from the trees. The light was filtered from a sun that did not appear.

I called the next man on guard and went back to my hole. I peeled off my overshoes, my boots and socks, and rubbed my freezing feet. Then I put on a pair of dry socks and my shoes and overshoes, and set about making breakfast. I

113

tore open the K-ration box, emptied it, and tore the box in strips. I mixed the strips with some dry twigs in a pile. I poured water into my mug, placed it on the twigs, and emptied the packet of coffee powder into it. I lit the pile. While the coffee was heating, I opened the can of egg-and-meat compound and ate this with the fortified biscuits.

It was then that the shells came in. They were falling around us. The ground shook and fragments of iron went singing by.

Being shelled is the real work of an infantry soldier, which no one talks about. Everyone has his own way of going about it. In general, it means lying face down and contracting your body into as small a space as possible. In novels you read about soldiers, at such moments, fouling themselves. The opposite is true. As all your parts are contracting, you are more likely to be constipated.

When the shelling stopped I got up, laid my rifle across the parapet pointing downhill, and looked around. Here and there the snow was blotched black, and the trees were gashed. Other helmets, like turtles, were stirring just above ground level. Someone shouted "Medic!" and the medics went forward, running in a crouch.

We stayed looking into the mist. Hours passed and it grew colder. I kept my hands clenched in my pockets to warm them, and stamped my feet.

That was the defence of Bastogne—standing in a hole in the snow, or lying down in the snow, for hours and days.

There was a flurry of rifle shots on the left of our position. A machine-gun opened up. Then from in front came the smooth purring of a German machine-gun. At the foot of the slope, among the trees and mist, were scarely visible flittings. I aimed at these movements and fired. The men around me were also firing. All at once the firing stopped. A voice was wailing in the trees. Then this too stopped. When I looked carefully I could see three bodies just beyond the trees. They were camouflaged in white cloaks and hoods.

The wind lifted the snow in skirts, sifting over the bodies. They became mounds on the surface. Light faded and the temperature fell. The nights, also, must be lived through.

★

In the middle of the night I was shaken awake by the First Sergeant.

"The Captain wants you."

I was the Captain's runner. I found him in a barn behind the hill. He was a small man who performed his duties precisely and without enthusiasm, like a dentist. He was not a pal to the troops; on the other hand, he had not made any fatal mistakes. He wanted me to carry a message to Battalion C.P. The message was oral: "G Company needs mortar ammunition. This is urgent. Also an anti-tank gun or tank-destroyer, if possible." I repeated the message.

"Watch out," said the First Sergeant, "there may be Krauts between here and Battalion."

I plodded off, making my way between trees shining with icicles. My feet were sore. If I ran into a German patrol I would fall on my elbows and start shooting. Beyond that my ideas were vague.

Being a runner gave you a chance to move around; and, however humbly, you had something to do with the intelligence that directed battles, if intelligence there was. At least I could figure out directions. My company was on the south-east of the perimeter; Battalion C.P. was between us and Bastogne. I drew a line in the air and followed it. And then I was sure to run into other men who would point me on. But I would have to keep listening for the word "Halt!" and stop when I heard it. Otherwise a runner could get shot.

I came to a road. About twenty yards away stood a Sherman tank, its seventy-five aiming down the road. A

man was sitting in the turret. I walked over. The man in
the turret, a staff-sergeant, looked down at me in silence,
then continued his perusal of the road. Where it turned, a
German tank was tilted into the ditch. Flames were licking
around the tank; it was the colour of mustard except where
it was scorched black. Its eighty-eight hung sideways, pointing into a snow-bank.

I waved a hand and continued my journey. I had every
confidence in the sergeant and his crew. But what if the
German tanks broke through here, behind our company? I
didn't ponder the question. It was abstract.

Battalion C.P., in a farmhouse blacker than night, was a
meeting-place for questions and rumours. We pressed close
to the stove.

"Where," said a p.f.c., "are our fuggin planes?"

"They can't see through the fog."

"They could drop some fuggin food at least. And pretty
soon we're goin' be outta fuggin ammo. An' if you're
wounded you could as well freeze to death."

"I hear they got Krauts disguised like G.I.'s."

"At St.-Vith they run over the line with tanks. SS
troops—they don't take no prisoners."

"Hey, you guys, we're surrounded!"

"Where'd you hear that?"

"Pucci heard it, over to Regiment."

A sergeant entered, stamping the snow off his boots.
Someone who knew him shouted, "Is it true we're surrounded?"

He assured us that we were.

It was almost a relief to get back to the optimists in the
foxholes. I reported that there were a few mortar shells in
supply; the company could send a detail to pick them up;
there were no anti-tank guns or tank-destroyers to be
spared; and the division was surrounded. Then I went back
to my sleeping bag.

Suddenly the fog lifted and the sun shone. Planes appeared
—ours—Thunderbolts, Typhoons, Spitfires. They dived;
rockets plunged down from their wings. They machine-
gunned the forest around us.

On Christmas Eve a messenger appeared to the companies:
"Any of you guys want to go to religious service?"

There were sudden conversions. Files of men were making
their way to the rear where the shelling wasn't so heavy.
We were on the outskirts of Bastogne. Some of the houses
had been flattened. During the nights we had heard German
planes droning over; somewhere behind us bombs whistled
and exploded and the ground trembled. This was where
the bombs had fallen.

The services were being held in a chapel. The Chaplain
spoke of Christmas. Things were tough here, especially
when you thought of holly and turkey and cranberry sauce.
But we were fighting against the forces of evil, protecting
our loved ones at home, so that the life represented by
Christmas might continue.

On Christmas Day the Germans bombarded us with
heavy artillery. They seemed to have some extra grievance.
The attack was no longer general but directed against each
one of us personally.

There were mechanical sounds in front of our position—
a whining of engines and clanking of treads. But no tanks
came up our way. They attacked elsewhere. The trees were
lit with red flames; pillars of smoke rose to join the grey-
white overcast.

My feet, by this time, were numb lumps. I limped
through the woods carrying messages—reports of the
company's strength, requests for ammunition, medical
supplies, something to stop tanks with.

Journeying to another company with a question about
our fields of fire, I passed a litter of dead Germans. They
were clamped in rigid attitudes—a fist or knee raised in the

air, eyes shining like discs of glass. Around them were the pieces of paper that surround dead soldiers, and enemy equipment—coal-scuttle helmets, cylindrical gas-mask containers, bolt-operated rifles, Schmeissers. These things, in their rust, showed how vastly the men who had oiled and polished them no longer cared.

We heard that we were no longer surrounded. Patton with his tanks had broken through the German ring.

We stayed where we were, and the shelling continued for days and nights. But the days were sun-warmed; icicles fell from the trees and snow began to melt. Extra boxes of rations were distributed.

One day when I reported to the Captain, trying to walk without using my feet, the First Sergeant stared at me and said, "You're going out."

I was in a line of invalids; then I lay in an ambulance, muffled in blankets. The ambulance moved. I had almost forgotten that men had invented things for their convenience, as well as high-explosive.

And now I was in a hospital bed in Paris, feet nakedly exposed to the temperature of the room. More than half the cases in the hospital had frozen feet. The rest were shell wounds, a few bullet wounds, fatigue.

I learned nothing about the battle from my fellow invalids. We didn't want to discuss what we had seen. At that time, anything beyond a gripe would have seemed like extravagant boasting. But we read *Time* and *Yank* and *Stars and Stripes* avidly, and what's more, we believed what we read. If Jimmy Cannon reported a "doughboy" as saying "Well, they have us surrounded, the poor bastards!" perhaps the man *did* say it, and we liked to think we would have said it, too.

Our battle passed into print and history and the movies. There would come a day when we would not be able to distinguish between true and false; we would not remember what war was like. That would be for another generation to discover.

THE BATTLE

Helmet and rifle, pack and overcoat
Marched through a forest. Somewhere up ahead
Guns thudded. Like the circle of a throat
The night on every side was turning red.

They halted and they dug. They sank like moles
Into the clammy earth between the trees.
And soon the sentries, standing in their holes,
Felt the first snow. Their feet began to freeze.

At dawn the first shell landed with a crack.
Then shells and bullets swept the icy woods.
This lasted many days. The snow was black.
The corpses stiffened in their scarlet hoods.

Most clearly of that battle I remember
The tiredness in eyes, how hands looked thin
Around a cigarette, and the bright ember
Would pulse with all the life there was within.

XXIII

Somewhere in Germany
March 1, 1945

This is the life! We lounge around in apartments and lean out of windows waving to each other.

We got here a week ago. "That", said the Major, "is the River X, and this is the Town of Y." He informed us that the houses going down to the water were our O.P.'s and the hotels back in town were our main line of resistance.

The password is comfort, and under these conditions war seems tolerable, almost normal. Each squad has its own house or rooms in a hotel on the main drag. In our house there are closets, tables, double beds, a library specializing in the exploits of the *Luftwaffe* in Poland. In short, all the conveniences of German housekeeping. Here I sit and, except for inspections, am free to write letters and puff on my pipe, glancing now and then at the knees of the jail-bait bicycling by.

A smoky sky hangs over the river, a meerschaum sky. We drink our German beer out of steins decorated with roses or big stomachs and comical German noses. Between drinks we wonder about the fellows on the other bank where our artillery is walking up and down.

There are lots of chess-sets, and I sit playing chess wth Lieutenant Reed, who has replaced Delminer, while every now and then the sky over the river blackens in one spot and spreads out the streamers of an explosion. First the flash, silver-white and red, the tinsel streamers, then a drifting smudge.

Othello's occupation is guard duty. When it's your turn there's a knock on the door and you roll out of the sheets. When your time's up you go to the room across the hall, where there's a "Do Not Disturb" sign on the door, and knock politely for your successor. That's the kind of war it's been lately. The replacements think this is the way it's always been. They look puzzled if you say "the churchyard at Veghel". The ones who really knew what the names meant died in the fullness of their knowledge. Between two men in a hole who are knocked down by a shell, and one of them is wounded and the other isn't . . . or between

120

a man who is wounded and a man who dies . . . there's an enormous difference. Well, it doesn't do to think too much about such things; to continue living is to be ignorant.

We are enjoying this respite while it lasts. The men who sit here, rifle leaning against a bureau, helmet hanging from a towel hook, may remember this as a blessed state—victory and the spoils of war. You must win, that's the only requirement. It's a requirement our enemies were able to meet for a long time.

You ride into a town, and the moment the tail-gate of the truck clangs open the world's your oyster. The fear the defeated show of your arms seems to be a fear of you. Who isn't seduced? The road back, withdrawal from the invasion, could be as dangerous as the road in. It isn't just surplus tanks and rusty cans that are left on the beaches of the world, but parts of men. Some Americans will never find their way back from these days of irresponsible power in which any decision they make, any quick word or bullet they release, is backed up by an army. So we sow the dragon's teeth.

Your town house, right under the nose of the brass, may not be too exciting, but the O.P.'s are another world. They're in the large houses, each with a wall around it, with lawns in front going down to the Rhine. Usually there's an orchard on the town side of the house and a garage with one or two cars.

Go into one of these mansions. Say the one in which a light machine-gun is set up. Approach on the last asphalted street, then turn toward the river, taking a path through a cabbage garden, ducking where breaks in the walls could show you to the watchers on the other bank. You don't want to attract the mortar shells which are on top of you without warning. It's two o'clock in the afternoon, town and water twinkling, and the cabbages, turnips and radishes give off a strong smell.

Through a hole in a wall you enter the orchard. Nothing's

121

good to eat on the vines at present. You climb some steps made of rock; then there's a square of grass with a concrete ping-pong table and a swimming pool. There's a little summer-house, too, with a double bed and, on shelves painted blue, a complete family of hand-carved yodellers. It's a haunting reminder of *gemütlichkeit*. The girls with strong legs and small breasts, and the young men with guitars slung across their shoulders, have departed. On the far bank the Siegfrieds watch the Rhine, nursing their burp-guns, and God knows what the maidens are up to. Many of them will never come back to the summer-house.

We're gripped with curiosity about these people. To have a souvenir at all costs! A hundred times a day the men expose themselves to death in the search. There's Fritz's dinner on the table, the meat congealed into lumps of iron. There's a record on the phonograph and a reel in the movie projector. You turn over the leaves of the photograph album in order to know the face which, for as long as you can remember, has filled your thoughts—the face of the enemy, which flies before you always.

Wanting to get as close as possible to the one you hate, the one who's done his level best to kill you—it's a strange attraction. The most powerful, perhaps, of all attractions. There's a dream I've had about it. I'm holding a hag in my arms. In spite of her stinking breath, her creaking joints, my revulsion, I press her closer to me. And because of my persistence—for I have a premonition that this will happen— suddenly she changes into one of those creatures who leave your heart palpitating a lifetime.

A charm is thrown over you when you enter an abandoned house. In the attic there may a blue-eyed maiden, a princess locked in a tower around which the dragon Thou-Shalt-Not-Fraternize romps and roars, carrying off many an unlucky wight to a court martial. Who will dare to free her and receive the kiss and the words with which, in a delicious, guttural, foreign language, the fair reward the brave? "*Ich liebe dich!*"

The boys aren't just after souvenirs when they knock over a book-shelf or slash a painting with a bayonet. They want to get at the precious answer they're sure is hidden somewhere. Their own country has told them nothing . . . perhaps the enemy will. A souvenir is part of your enemy, left behind in his flight as Grendel left his arm and shoulder haunch in Beowulf's hands when he went howling to his den under the marshes. Even a booby-trap—which looters claim as their excuse for overturning a bureau drawer on the floor or knocking in a grandfather clock—is fascinating. It represents the still beating heart, the detached but still working brain of the enemy. Taking it apart you could discover what makes the Germans tick.

Looters don't collect property because they want it. They lose diamond rings easily. They know they can't carry half the stuff they cram into ammo bags. Looting is . . . exciting. So's the whole business—there's nothing more exciting than an advance. We would like the advance and retreat to continue indefinitely. And there'll be thousands of men who won't want to give up the good hunting. After the war, what will they do? Will America be a nation of scavengers? And government be the problem of loot?

There's savagery in this kind of war; just enough comfort has been let in to make the men recall their lives at home and resent the discomforts they still have to put up with. The nursery upstairs was opened to the weather by a shell, but the drawing-room has received no more mercy from the invaders. Everywhere there are eloquent blanks. Here a picture has been removed, here a dozen pages have been torn out of a book and the book thrown to the floor. A trail of stamps shows by which door a collection has departed, probably to be left in a ditch when an eighty-eight opens up.

The boys are sitting around in the dining-room with their feet on the shining mahogany table, eating their miserable biscuits and corned pork loaf garnished with onions.

"Captain, is it true the outfit's pulling out tomorrow?"

They're hoping for new towns to conquer—across the Rhine, across the Danube, deeper and deeper in. Can the machine that brought them so far ever take them back? With so many sharp turns in the road, with so many precipices, so many accidents, what chance they'll ever see home again? You tell them you never listen to rumours and hand them their letters. They snatch eagerly at the scrawls from America. They wish they were home. They grin and laugh as they read, lost in the words as in a pleasant dream. Their absorption and starts of joy make them look like idiots to the men who got no letters. These sit at the window, their hands on the tripod of the machine-gun, watching the far bank. That's where the enemy is. Over there's the untaken town and the loot. Tomorrow . . .

And because the shells are bursting over there, the air we breathe is sweeter.

XXIV

When Germany surrendered the regiment was stationed in Berchtesgaden. After the grubbiness of France, the autobahns and clean, modern building seemed like home. The fräuleins were blonde, and our officers were pleased by the respect that Germans had for officers, of whatever army. They felt that in order to impress the Germans we should show that we were as well-disciplined as the *Waffen SS*, so there was much cleaning of equipment and we paraded the roads in perfect formations.

We were ordered to have a regimental newspaper, and I was put in charge. Then the regiment moved from Berchtesgaden to Sens in France. Here we set up the newspaper again. Every few days we would discover that we had run out of paper and had to take a truck into Paris to get more rolls. We would drive in early, park the truck, and disperse, meeting again late that night to drive back to Sens. We spent the day reeling from one bar to another.

I made no connection between all I had read about Paris and my present surroundings. At the end of the war, culture no longer existed, and if a friend had asked me to come along and meet Picasso, and another friend had asked me to have a drink, I wouldn't have hesitated—I would have made for one of the bars at the foot of Sacré Coeur. There I leaned against the counter, with a cigar stuck in my face, putting down one cognac after another. There was no shortage of cognac and our pockets were full of money. Our back pay had caught up with us all at once. Our supplies also had reached us, and every day someone threw another carton of cigarettes on to my bed, and this could be converted on the black market into thousands of francs.

In the bars women stuck to our money like flies. These women were young and some of them were attractive. They were prostitutes, but then so many of the women of France at this time were prostitutes that the word had lost its meaning. It was just what women were doing at the end of the war.

At Sens I met a young woman who was not a prostitute. She was slender and rather pretty, with a humorous way of talking. She wore her hair cut very short, in a style that would later be called Italian. I took her out a few times, and then a friend asked if I had noticed her peculiar haircut. He explained that she was one of the women who had been friendly with the Germans and had had her head shaved by patriotic Frenchmen. This cooled my interest in young ladies of good families.

*

We were shipped home from Marseilles. My last view of Europe was significant. In the midst of piles of rubble a German prisoner-of-war was operating a crane, sorting out the concrete blocks and broken pieces of iron. The German was the only energetic human being in sight.

I was discharged from the army at Fort Dix, and remember a colonel addressing us and telling us that some day we would look back on these as the best days of our lives. I have no doubt that for the colonel and other officers the war had indeed been the best experience of their lives. Certainly the post-war history of the United States indicates this. All that those of us who were in the infantry, tanks and planes wanted was to get it over with and get out. We could hardly wait to be discharged. But what did the colonels have to go back to? And the generals and admirals? In wartime conditions they were important and when they gave an order thousands of men hastened to carry it out. Their beds were made for them every morning, they ate well, and women flattered them. In contrast to this, in civilian life they would have to hold down a job that was no sinecure; they would be competing against other men, and ability would be required. At home they would be nagged by their wives and bothered by their children. So these men, after the war, would try to perpetuate the conditions of war, and in collaboration with the manufacturers of arms and the politicians, they would change

126

the United States from the generous, imaginative, somewhat comical nation that it had been—a nation of have-nots—into the military nation, riddled with fear and distrust, that it now is.

3

XXV

When I got back New York was strange and the people I
talked to seemed to have no concept of reality—that is, the
sight of blood. I suffered from the condition described by
Robert Graves and familiar to many an ex-infantryman: at
every street corner, and when I passed an open place, I would
look for a machine-gun position; at any whistling sound or
bang my whole body would convulse.

I was readmitted at Columbia, and set about reading
Aquinas and other philosophers.

At the same time I was writing stories about the war.

When he saw her he knew that he was fascinated. The
close-cropped skull, the sharp profile of an aristocrat, the
brilliant morbid eyes, and above all her devilish laugh . . .
How could he resist them. One might as well try to
walk over an enemy's body without looking at it, without
examining the wounds.

He invited her to drink.

Her teeth were very even, and he noticed that she was
clean, with the scrupulous cleanliness of a person who is
inwardly dirty. She drank nothing stronger than beer, and
warned him against his calvados, which, she pointed out,
would be bad for him. The price too, she said, was a
scandal.

He began to drink fast and straight, which was his way
of getting to the point with the least trouble.

He got there in an hour: it used to take longer.

She cried easily, and told him that she had no family,
that the doors were locked to her, that her child was
starving, that she had no one to care for her.

And as suddenly, she stopped, remarking with a sly grin: "*Alles ist kaputt!*"

The transition from French to German was so quick that he didn't register at once how that made everything stick together. He put his hand up to her short curls and he knew that she was one of them, the collaborators, the shaven-heads.

He ordered another drink.

Darkness had closed in, and his time was running out.

"Look," he said, "*Venez ici! Six heures demain, six heures. J'aurai toute la nuit.*"

But at six o'clock the next day he was crammed into one of the "cattle trucks", and on his way to the front.

★

"Were they good to you in the hospital?" she asked.

"Yes, very good. The American Army has finer medical equipment than any other army."

He was extremely formal. Lazarus had probably spoken grammatically and made classic gestures when he was informed of his new lease on life.

The soldier lifted his glass stiffly. He studied the amber liquid.

"It is six o'clock," she said. "Do you remember? Two months ago to the day."

"I remember."

"Look," she said, "my hair is longer now. You can wind it around your fingers."

He looked at that beautiful face with curiosity.

"See," she said, "touch it."

He wound one of the curls around his forefinger. It was silky.

"Did you kill many of the Boches?" she said. "It was very fine. We read all about it."

"Come with me," he said, coldly.

Her dark eyes lingered in his.

"*Quand même*," she whispered, "you soldiers . . ."

"What do you mean?"

"The French," she said, "Germans, Americans . . . you are all the same."

He got up and reached for his hat. His anger was so great he was afraid he might hit her. Outside in the darkness again he heard a violin playing, and he smiled.

"*Auprès de ma blonde*," he sang, which was the only song in a foreign language he knew.

This reads like a parody. The thing that strikes me now about this sort of writing is how untrue it was. I think this is characteristic of most people who want to be writers: they want to write a story or poem—they don't care about telling the truth. A regard for truth comes later; it is the last flower of a lifelong devotion—but in the beginning all that matters is to astonish people.

So my real experiences of the war were falsified. The style was Hemingway and I was being a tough guy. Young men who have no sense of their identity are given to striking tough attitudes. This goes hand in hand with sentimentality about women, which appears as cynicism. It is all just defensive.

In my case, however, there was some reason to be bitter. Sorrows remembered from childhood were coming with a rush to the surface. In my case, the struggle and release from the mother that occurs in adolescence had not occurred. How can you be free of a mother who is not there? I had not killed my dragon, and until I did I would not be able to marry the princess.

★

I was seeing Bonnie again. I felt a wonderful excitement,

knowing that I was on my way to see her, that within a few minutes, when I rang the doorbell, I would hear her steps approaching, and in a few seconds she would be standing before me.

Since I had gone into the army Bonnie had grown up. With her black curls, her curved figure and coquettish ways, a hundred years ago she would have been "the rage of the park, the ball-room, the opera and the croquet lawn". In this day and age the effect was that of a stand-in for some movie-star—I couldn't be sure which.

The apartment she lived in was cluttered with furniture and bric-à-brac, and her parents were equally stuffy, seeing that I came to take out their Bonnie without wearing a tie. Bonnie bit her lip—she couldn't wait to get me out of there. I was genuinely puzzled. What was the matter?

I took her to dinner and a movie, and afterwards asked her to marry me. I forget what she said, but the answer was no. I forget, also, what I said—for we are now entering a period of amnesia—but I imagine I shrugged, said something worldly—"Ça m'est égal!" and turned on heel and strode away.

Having been rejected by love, I returned to art. It was with me as with Madame Blavatsky: "I write, write, write as the Wandering Jew walks, walks, walks."

For weeks I hardly slept or ate. I read furiously, making my brains feverish with metaphysics. I was perplexed by religion; I worried about Jesus; at the same time I was conscious of being a Jew.

In retrospect, this makes the man I then was seem distant, almost a stranger, to the man I am now. For though I have religious impulses and sometimes look back with nostalgia upon evenings in the school chapel and the singing of hymns, I am not troubled by questions of theology.

There was a shadow standing at the periphery of vision.... When I looked it would flit away.

It seems that I heard voices.

The stairs asked why I was returning so soon. I looked in every pocket, and couldn't find the key. A few hours later someone came across me lying in the corridor—this must be true for they say so and I don't remember. I became violent, and made speeches, and had to be taken away in an ambulance.

Ted Hoffman came to see me in the hospital. We had been out of touch for some time. He says:

> I hardly saw you, having myself left to face marriage at Harvard . . . having endured a strange hospital year of two delicate long operations, and a bout with death, all the while feeling guilty about friends who could only boast of *pieds gelés* and shrapnel in the buttocks. . . . I left you there ensconced at Columbia, boy poet turned tough, knocking off a $300 article for *Esquire*, turning out the novel Maxwell Perkins was waiting for the secretary to bring in the door . . . ready to preside over the heritage of the new hip drug crowd I'd left you.
>
> Why weren't you happy resuming that education? I was not disturbed when my brother (whom you roomed with in my apartment) was puzzled at your inference that the seal in the Central Park Zoo knew more of the nature of life than he would ever understand; he was willing to forgive poets. What surprised me was to discover when you had descended into West End Avenue to demonstrate God's wishes to men of any will and only encountered policemen with billys aimed at your mouth and they took you away, that it was I who was your friend. I was shocked. It was a betrayal. You were to make it, I to slide into confusion.

Ted, as you see, was thrown by my "nervous breakdown", and, looking over his account of the period, I recall what I have forgotten; the worst thing about being ill is that you put other people to so much trouble on your account. It's the shame you never get over. Huck Finn enjoyed going to his own funeral and listening to all the nice things people said about him, and the psychologists tell us that this is a common fantasy. But I must be the opposite of Huck, for I hated my funeral.

Ted came to see me at the hospital where I was incarcerated.

I took you on, not as a burden, as a kind of mission, feeling that I had studied with Simpson, not Columbia; surely I'd learned more cutting classes to look up what you talked about than if I'd looked up what they talked about (except Weaver; the true dowsing rod of wisdom). Actually, I only visited you a few times, stupidly calling your mother weekly for permission, she suggesting I'd better wait, obviously (maybe sensibly) frightened of those conversations you would hold with me.

By then, I could handle you. I could even review the day clearly on that sweltering Long Island Railroad trip back to NY. I knew what it meant to meet Proust's ex-chauffeur in a bar in Paris, to return to NY and inform Mark Van Doren, when he noted on a *Tempest* paper you were pushing contemporary allusions too much, that the Garden of Eden was NOW! (which he naturally agreed with, and would today or any day, as he would agree to anything anyone with talent or genius or maybe even just love for anything would say), and that the reason was that technology had destroyed time so that all lives ever lived were being lived simultaneously, which was why you could ask Walter Adams for his watch, throw it out the window and remark we didn't need such instruments any more.

Well, as I say, by that time we were both very well educated, and I could take that out to the hospital and subsume it under a discussion. (I'm sure we did a turn or two with Hamlet and the middle Shakespeare, and Prospero and those who have power but. They were great afternoons out there, with your mother interpreting all your spiel as a desire to break loose, command the LIRR and rape Fay Wray on the Empire State Building.) I have the memory of instinctively believing that you, nutty as a fruit-cake—man you were, with each successive treatment—were capable still of philosophic discourse at the highest level.

Research subsequent to those days, the theory of which interests Lynn, indicates that if you induced the pigs to knock out your front teeth with tales of angels on high, the welfare system was geared to board you on LI for from six to nine months with various chemical aids, depending how long it took you to surrender rhetoric for plain talk. Had you assaulted the policeman without the rhetoric, or limited yourself to simple scatological and fornicative and sodomistic epithets, you would have been released sooner. But our society gets you on grounds of imagery, metaphor, etc., at least that which is not in the multimedia catechism. So I did not try to explain to your mother why you kept bugging her to buy you a new wrist-watch when you immediately smashed every one she bought you, and I did not say anything when I got to talk to your psychiatrist (yours and 900 other guys) and when I asked him how all this would affect your writing he (1) expressed surprise you had ever been capable of writing, and (2) urged me not to expect any of *that* again.

★

When I came out of my fog I was surrounded by lunatics, in a room with bars on the windows. Outside the world went merrily on, while in these walls men and women howled, brayed, and maioued. There was very little psychiatric care; the running of the place was left to the guards. I recollect one instance of their care-taking. I had become friends with a Negro boy in my ward, and he came toward me holding out a newspaper. "Read this for me, will ya?" he said. One of the guards was standing close by and, out of sheer lightmindedness, the boy turned and struck him on the chest. The guard knocked the boy down, then another guard came running up, and the two guards stood over the boy kicking him in the ribs and belly.

The next day one of the other attendants—a Negro—told me the boy had died and asked me if I would testify before the hospital authorities about what I'd seen. I said that I would. But soon I was visited by one of the guards who had killed the boy, and he told me, "If you say a thing about yesterday, we'll have you put in the violent ward and you'll be there for the rest of your life." I have no doubt that he could have done it. I did not testify, and was released from the hospital in due time.

People who have not been through such experiences cannot be made to understand through words what they are like. The worst thing is not the spectacle of insanity nor the brutality. I had had my front teeth knocked out, and had been set upon by a guard who was drunk, but I really didn't mind it. I had seen worse things during the war. In Holland I had to walk every night through a field where American and German soldiers had fought at close range. The field was covered with their bodies in every conceivable attitude, swelling and splitting. I walked through this field by moonlight for several weeks, carrying messages to battalion headquarters, and grew accustomed to sights of violence and death. But the hospital showed me something beyond death—hell, the disconnection of the self from the universe. When you have lost your mind and still you continue to exist . . . well, it's pathetic.

My experiences in the hospital left me with a lack of sympathy for the everyday "problems" of human beings. I cannot take people's troubles in love too seriously, and am unable to sympathize as I ought with a man who has difficulties finishing a job. As for people who think there is something romantic about mental disorder, I must confess I have contempt for them. A misfortune such as I have been describing need not make a man better and more intelligent, it may simply harden him and make him impatient and, worst of all, kill his joy in life.

In my mind there has always been an odd comparison between the mental hospital and the actions of the Germans during the war. The final harm that the Germans did was to damage mankind's confidence in its own essential goodness. When the Germans created Belsen and Buchenwald they made it impossible for mankind to think so well of itself again. Since that time men have somehow despised themselves—that is, thinking men. Nothing that people do in the future—not even if another Jesus came—could make up for the disgusting cruelties perpetrated on men, women and children in the concentration camps. Mankind has lost its sense of connection with ultimate good. My stay in the hospital showed me what it was to lose one's sense of connection and no longer be able to trust one's fellow man. I had an idea of what it must have been like to be in the concentration camps, and nothing that happened afterwards would make life seem necessarily good.

A psychiatrist could find several reasons for my break-down, going back to my childhood. This has been an age of psychiatry. But while we have tipped the balance toward sociological, psychological and biological explanations of man's behaviour, in reaction against centuries during which only man's spiritual life was examined, in our time we have over-compensated so that we have forgotten that ideas are realities—gods, as the Greeks used to think. At the time of my illness I was hallucinating, and I am not willing to think that these hallucinations had no value. One episode in particular strikes me as significant. In this moment my own trouble and my ideas about the Jews came together with a supernatural clarity.

We had been having a therapeutic session of painting and drawing under the guidance of a woman. I did an oil painting of trees, grass, clouds, and she was pleased; she called the doctor to look at it. We hardly ever saw the doctor, but he happened to be passing through. But the next picture I drew was different— a drawing of the ward with the patients sitting in depressed positions and with a swastika on the wall. When she looked at this she was silent, then she said, "Well, the light isn't good now."

A little later I was standing on the porch, looking out through the bars at the Sound. Around me were other patients—the one who lay face down on a bench, contracting, the four who were always playing cards. Then I heard, as distinctly as I have ever heard anything, a voice say "Praise God! They resist, they resist."

Who resisted? What were they resisting? I wish that I knew.

Lazarus Convalescent

These are the evening hours and he walks
Down to the Hudson, to that lonesome river,
And while a piano plays he sits and talks . . .
"Do you remember Judson?
Huge cloudy symbols of a high romance.
I think he went into insurance."

The water laps, the seagulls plunge and squawk
And lovers lock in wind that makes him shiver.
"I'll have to learn to use a knife and fork
Again. Look there above us!

Spry's for Baking . . . starry spectacle.
For Frying. More, a miracle."

Perhaps at running water he can balk
The bloodhound that is howling for his liver.
Now will he rise again, rise up and walk.
"And do you know, I've found
My neighbours spy on me when I undress.
Perhaps I ought to change, to change my address."

He sees his oracle, the weight machine.
His flesh is right; he laughs and pats the giver.
Alas, its entrails also tell his fortune,
Turning him ghastly white.
He moves from all his friends with a cursed stealth.
What has the mouth informed him? "Guard your health."

XXVI

After the hospital I had an obsession—not to go back. I was
still unstable; for no apparent reason I would break into
cold sweats and feel that I was fainting.

Moreover, I had amnesia. I could not remember the
months preceding my collapse, or episodes of the war, or
my childhood. Sometimes I would start reading a book and,
half-way through, realize that I had read it before. When I
tried to write something, afterwards if I looked through my
old papers I would discover that I was repeating words and
lines and whole paragraphs I had written years before. In
order to recover the past I began simple exercises, pushing

back the fog. What did it look like, the lane that you lived on when you were a child? Where were the driveway and the garden? The veranda? When you went through the door into the living-room what did you see? I remembered a doll on a shelf that unscrewed at the middle so that there was another doll inside it, and that too could be unscrewed, and so on.

In this way I got the facts right, and developed an extreme respect for mere facts and the practical arrangement of things. I could not trust my feelings and was determined to have no opinions, for, it seemed, it was opinions that had got me into trouble—ideas about war, women, religion. From now on I would just pay attention to my buttons.

I therefore set myself a regime. I ate even when I didn't feel like it, and tried to get enough sleep.

I applied again at Columbia to finish my degree, and was told that I could register if I had the college doctor's permission. I went to see him. He picked up a folder from his desk and glanced through it. "You ought to get a job for a while," he said. "I think you ought to get to know the common man. And you won't be spending so much time on your music, will you?" For a moment I thought this was some sort of test of my sanity. I told him no, indeed, I wouldn't be spending so much time on my music. But the answer didn't work, for he did not give me permission. It was only months later that I realized he had been looking at the wrong file. How had the poor musician who came after me responded when he was told not to spend so much time reading books and writing poetry?

So I got a job downtown in the import-export business. In the evenings I wrote. I found that poetry was the only kind of writing in which I could express my thoughts and make some definite sense. I could start a poem and bring it to a conclusion within a short time, whereas prose required you to sustain a mood and train of thought, and I

142

couldn't. Through poems I could release the irrational, grotesque images I had accumulated during the war, and imposing order on these images enabled me to recover my identity. One night I dreamed that I was lying under machine-gun and mortar fire, and I wrote it out, and as I wrote I realized that it wasn't a dream, but a memory of being under fire.

So I began piecing the war together, and wrote poems about it: "Carentan O Carentan" and "Memories of a Lost War"—the early days of the fighting in Normandy; "The Battle"—the fighting at Bastogne. I wanted to recapture the atmosphere of war, to paint the landscape, to record the numbing of intellect and emotion, and the endurance of the American infantry soldier. I wanted each poem to be abrasive, like a pebble in a shoe.

To the foot-soldier, war is almost entirely physical. That is why some men, when they think about war, fall silent. Language seems a betrayal of physical life and a betrayal of those who have experienced it absolutely—the dead. As Hemingway remarked, to each man the names on a map are more significant than works of imagination.

In a post-war world, however, there are limitations to the dog-face way of looking at things. Love, for example, is not best written about by a man who is trying to avoid extra duty. And a country cannot be governed by silence and inertia. In recent years the close-mouthed, almost sullen, manner of my early poems has given way to qualities that are quite different. Like other men of the war generation I began with middle age; youth came later. Nowadays in poems I try to generate mystery and excitement; I have even dealt in general ideas. But I retain the dog-face's suspicion of the officer class, with their abstract language and indifference to individual, human suffering. The war made me a foot-soldier for the rest of my life.

What, in these poems, was I trying to do that had not

143

already been done? I did not wish to protest against war. Any true description of modern warfare is a protest, but many have written against war with satire and indignation, and it still goes on. My object was to witness and to record. I wanted people to find in my poems the truth of what this war had been like. I was writing a memorial of these years for the men I had known, who were silent. I was trying to write poems that I would not be ashamed to have them read—poems that would be, in their laconic and simple manner, tolerable to men who had seen a good deal of combat and had no illusions.

*

I got back into Columbia by a rear door, by way of the School of General Studies. I could take courses there in the evenings and get a degree. It was so that I met younger students and writers who had not been in the war and whose attitudes were new to me. There were others I met at parties in the Village and in cold-water flats on the East Side. One night I gave a party of my own—I was living on West End Avenue—to which came a number of my new friends, bringing friends of their own. There was a thin, sallow young man with staring eyes and a puzzling smile, Allen Ginsberg. He'd been at Columbia while I was away. There was a burly fellow with an all-American face, Jack Kerouac. Another named Neil Cassady. The party got rough and they threw glasses out of the window to shatter on the pavement ten floors below. Ginsberg appeared from my bedroom carrying the sheet of a poem I had been trying to write, tripping rhymes about a little German girl. He read it aloud to my embarrassment. It seemed that Ginsberg, too, was trying to write poetry, and Kerouac had written a novel comparing the city and the country.

The next day I found that a copy of Henry Miller's *Tropic*

of Cancer that I'd picked up in Paris was missing. I've sometimes thought that, in this small way, I contributed to the growth of the Beats.

There was a man named John Hollander who seemed to know everything about poetry, especially metrics, and music. He would sit at the piano playing T. S. Eliot—that is, singing the words of "The Waste Land" to an arrangement of his own. And Ted Hoffman was living on Barrow Street in the Village; he was specializing in theatre, mentioning names I'd never heard of—Bertolt Brecht and Eric Bentley.

There were a few girls who came to the parties, wild young things who had been educated at progressive schools. They were always talking about *avant-garde* painting and music and books. They dressed in hand-me-downs and came and went at odd hours.

I was invited to take part in a poetry-reading at Columbia. The other readers were Allen Ginsberg and John Hollander. The famous English poet Stephen Spender would make the introduction. Spender's name meant a great deal to me. He was one of the so-called Oxford poets—W. H. Auden, Stephen Spender, C. Day Lewis and Louis MacNeice. Many poets of the 'thirties and 'forties wrote in imitation of these men's style—a mixture of prep-school flippancy and private jokes—and borrowed their Marxist and Freudian attitudes, their symbolism of images taken from machinery. Spender's poems were quite sentimental, but they were bedecked with pylons, factory chimneys and locomotives. My own early poems had been alliterated like Auden's and brought up to date with Spenderesque references to machinery.

> Life is a winter liner, here history passes
> Like tourists on top-decks, seeing the shore through
> sun-glasses . . .

Introducing us, Spender said a few words about the poetry of the day. The main difference between English and

145

American poetry was that Englishmen had experienced the war and Americans hadn't. I listened to this description with some astonishment. Spender's other remarks were made with the same off-hand air of authority, and for the first time I began to wonder if famous English authors knew as much as they seemed to.

Ginsberg read some poems about North Africa; he'd been there on a boat as a member of the crew. Later we walked down the Drive together talking about poetry. It was a hard life. He showed me holes in the elbows of his jacket.

Ginsberg giggled a lot, but his writing was apocalyptic.

The land of our Forefathers has been, in history, compelled to a distinctly scatalogical habit, the fetishistic accumulation of mechanical knick-knacks, foorforaw, and plastic utilities as buttresses against reality; this, side by side with an even more patently scatalogical compulsion towards purity of convention and appearance. . . . All our healthiest citizens are at this very moment turning into hipsters, hop-heads, and poets. The state of the nation today, whether or not the proper authorities will recognize it, is one of complete anarchy, violent chaos, sado-masochistic bar-room confusion, and clinical hysteria, in which the megalopolitan mayors are continually trying to crusade against natural instincts, and unsuccessfully attempting to suppress every perversion and criminality consequent in original suppression and traumatic intimidation . . . . The awful consummation of this holocaust of hysterical irresponsibility is the Atom Bomb.

Ginsberg hasn't much changed, from that day to this. I doubt that people ever do change fundamentally. They may go off in directions that seem contrary, but in a while you see that these were only digressions; the main direction is unaltered. Twenty years later, people are pretty much what you might have expected them to be; it is the ways by which they have arrived that are astonishing.

In order to be true to themselves, poets have to go far afield and discover new ways of speaking. Apollinaire says:

Sacrifice taste and keep your sanity
If you love your home you must make a journey
You must cherish courage and seek adventure . . .
Don't hope for rest risk everything you own
Learn what is new for everything must be known . . .

The world does not see the necessity of this. But poets know that their most extravagant actions are dictated by a need to be perfectly simple.

XXVII

The Veterans' Administration decided that my breakdown had been due to combat fatigue. They gave me a pension and I bought a ship ticket to France. I wanted to put an ocean between myself and my illness. Besides, all American writers went to Paris, and I had a longing to see the city again—the days I spent there during the war had been just enough to whet my appetite.

When I arrived I registered for the Course in Civilization at the University of Paris. This would give me something to do.

The course was designed for Americans, especially ex-soldiers, whose dollars were needed immediately by the French. One part of the course was French composition, taught by a professor whose method was a triumph of that logic on which the French pride themselves. The professor would translate passages from French novels into English. The professor's English. Then we translated the passages back into French. Then he marked our efforts wrong, because they did not correspond, word for word, with the original, *le mot juste*.

I protested that the method, though logical, did not allow for the use of intelligence. The professor replied that Americans had no training in logic or taste, and moreover he was a professor of the University of Paris.

If I try, I can still hear him expounding the beauties of a passage by Anatole France. What made it beautiful? Could no one tell? It was a description of Paris, viewed from the famous author's window on the Seine. This was the art, that in describing things far away France had used fifty-seven syllables. Did anyone dispute the computation? No. Well, now look! In describing things seen close at hand, France had used twenty-two syllables, only twenty-two. What was the reason? Could no one tell? Mees Brown? Meester Smeeth? Meester . . . No one? Ah, there was a hand! A miracle. What, what was that? Yes, of course. The great author had used more syllables for things seen far away than for things seen close at hand because at a distance one sees many, many more things.

What seems to be the trouble? You seem to have an objection, Meester Smeeth. Well, if Meester Smeeth wishes to correct the method of the French masters, we should all give him our attention. What's that? I don't understand. No, not "oo" but "eou", with the lips held so. Not "et", Meester Smeeth, but "ay". You are saying?

"Suppose France was describing a house ten feet away, and the same house a kilometre away . . . I mean, isn't it possible that you see more details close at hand than at a distance? Or suppose he was describing a locomotive right

148

in front of him, and an empty field. Wouldn't the locomotive get more syllables?"

''Meester Smeeth, no nonsense, please. This is the way
Anatole France has written it. Listen."

The professor reads through the passage, giving full
expression to every word. Any questions? There are no
more questions. Nevertheless, he has it in for Smith, and
twenty minutes later swoops down to surprise him reading
a book under the desk. The professor holds the book up and
shakes it.

"Ah, very good! It is not even in French! *Lif on Ze
Meeseeseepi*! Very good, reading Engleesh novels during ze
class!"

Afterwards, Smith is called to the department office,
where he is warned that such behaviour, coupled with his
absences, may have a dire consequence—the cutting-off of
his GI Bill. . . .

Besides composition, we were taught Method. The class
was in the hands of a portly dame. She said that the classical
method of criticism was based on Taine. But before one
could approach Taine it would be necessary to review
French grammar. And before one could approach grammar
it would be necessary to learn the proper pronunciation of
the language. She approached with a lighted candle and held
it in front of a student's mouth. She asked him to pronounce
the vowels. If he exhaled while uttering the vowels, the
flame flickered. If his pronunciation was atrocious, the flame
went out.

"The lips like this . . . ooh! ooh! The tongue back so."

In front of me the flame writhed like a tortured creature
and died. I was reduced from an enthusiasm for French
literature to stuttering, and then to silence. Smith and I
spent more time at a table with a view of the Boul Mich
than we did in the classroom. However, once a week I
revisited Mademoiselle's class, and there they would be,

more than a score of adults groaning the vowels in unison or chanting the sentences of a primer for six-year-olds. Paris is worth a mass. These visits were necessary for me to be nominally included on the list of students and kept on the payroll at the American consulate.

Then I had an idea. Maybe I should quit the course for Americans and get into the classes for French students. I had noticed a course in Baudelaire advertised on the bulletin board. Baudelaire would be fun. There's no time like the present—why didn't I go over to the university and register for Baudelaire right now?

I went to the building where one registered. It was full of French and foreign students, but no Americans. The waiting line wound up a staircase. I took a place on the lowest stair. How earnest these students seemed! This was the real Sorbonne, certainly. The French students, in particular, looked in earnest. They made jokes among themselves—they'd probably known one another in the *lycée*—but whenever anything official happened—a door opening at the top of the stairs, a name being called—they grasped their books and riffled to attention. Going to school was very serious for French students. Their whole life could depend on the results of examinations.

At last I arrived at the top of the stairs, facing the door. A voice said, "*Entrez!*" I entered. A man in white, evidently a doctor, walked up to me. "Certificate of inoculation," he said.

"I beg your pardon?"

"The certificate of inoculation. It is necessary to have a certificate of inoculation in order to register. This is an institution of the state. Have you been inoculated against typhus and diphtheria?"

"I don't know," I said. "I suppose I must have been. At some time. I only want to take a course in Baudelaire."

"Then it is absolutely necessary that you be inoculated."

"Very well," I said.

The doctor filled a hypodermic needle. "Take off your jacket and shirt, if you please."

I did as I was told. He stepped behind me, and a moment later I felt as if I'd been shot with a gun.

"Jesus Christ!"

He stepped in front of me again. "You will return tomorrow."

I put on my shirt and jacket and went downstairs. In half an hour I was lying on my bed in my hotel room. My temperature was rising, and when I dozed off I had the fitful dreams of fever. My back, where the doctor had driven the needle in, was throbbing. I dreamed of water and ice, pitchers of lemonade. I woke with a parched mouth and throbbing head, to see night falling outside. At a window opposite, an old woman was gazing out at the dusk like some terrible bird of prey. I'll bet they live on soup, she and her family; the soup of horse bones. I need iced lemonade.

It was a bad night, but the next morning my temperature was down. Once more I set off for the Sorbonne, to complete my registration.

Again I stood in line on the staircase. When I arrived at the top, the same voice said, "*Entrez.*"

"Ah yes," said the doctor. "Now, the inoculation, eh?"

"Wait a moment," I said. "I had an injection yesterday."

"There are three injections. This is the second."

He filled the hypodermic needle and I took off my jacket and shirt. This time, when he stepped behind me, I thought I knew what to expect and braced myself accordingly. But the shock was no less, nor the pain.

"Holy Mother of God!"

Three hours later I was tossing on my bed in delirium. The Sahara, dry as a bone, stretched to the horizon. An Arab on a camel came riding by. He had a big goatskin of cold

151

water flapping at his side. When I asked him for a drink he stopped obligingly. But, just as I was raising the goatskin to my lips, the camel put his head round and tried to take a bite out of my back. The camel and rider vanished. I was standing on the staircase, next to a French student who had his face in a book. "How many inoculations are there?" I asked him. Without taking his head out of the text he said, "What course do you wish to take?" "Baudelaire," I said. He did not answer, but whispered to someone standing on the other side. The whisper travelled up the staircase. The door at the top flew open and a voice shouted, "Baudelaire, three injections!"

The next day, instead of going to the university, I sat down at a table at the Flore and thought things over. Then I tore up the application forms.

After all, this was what Baudelaire would have done. Or was it? French writers, even the decadents, are sticklers for rules; *au fond*, most of them are middle-class. In fact, France has no poets of the first rank. I decided to give up French poetry and read the Russians in translation.

XXVIII

I lived for a year in France, and published a book of poems.

At my own expense.

No book is ever as exciting as the first. I was on my way back to my hotel with the galleys, long sheets of heavy paper, when I passed a Frenchman, a bookseller I knew, standing in the door of his establishment.

"Look," I said, showing him the galleys.

"What have you got there?"

"My book."

"What sort of book?"

"Poems."

He took the heavy galleys and, thoughtfully, weighed them in his hands. "Poetry," he said, "should be light. It should fly."

This was the first review I received. The second was a remark by John Hollander. "Interesting," he said. "It reminds me of Wyatt. But minor. It's minor poetry."

There was another notice of the book, far away in Jamaica. The reviewer said that I had left my origins far behind, to live in New York and travel in Europe. I had become cynical. He urged me to come back to the island and sit on a hill in the sunshine, "singing my native songs".

But I had no wish to return to Jamaica. From time to time I wondered what my life would have been like had I stayed there, and whenever I came across these lines by Scott I felt a twinge of uneasiness:

> Breathes there the man with soul so dead,
>   Who never to himself hath said,
>   This is my own, my native land!

Yet, though I had been born in Jamaica, the island now seemed further away than Russia, where my mother's people came from. The memories of my childhood were faint; they lay on the other side of a curtain—the war. It was as though I had been melted down, new-stamped and cast. I dated my life from the time that I had had to defend it.

★

I came back to New York. For a while I tried just writing, but every morning I could hear the city "going to work"—

and I wasn't. It didn't help to think that many businessmen didn't actually do anything. I still felt guilty. As Coolidge said, "The business of America is business." I was living against the grain, the stream of commercial life. I felt that I had to get a job.

At that time, after the war, people wanted security. They wanted steady jobs and comfortable houses. The veterans of the war were too tired to protest about anything; they were a "silent generation".

So runs the familiar thesis. Let us take it a little further.

The children of this generation were brought up permissively. For it was the easiest way to bring up children. They were given anything they liked, for their parents were too tired to say no. Or perhaps the parents didn't have any ideas of their own, or didn't love their children enough. Consequently, when the children came of age they would despise the parents and all authority. They would be the dropouts, flower children, and campus rebels of the 'sixties.

I'll go along with the thesis. The fact that it has been stated frequently and most people accept it doesn't mean that it's wrong. I think that the vision we have of the 'fifties, a Levittown inhabited by breeding couples who had no ideas beyond their own lives, "interpersonal relationships", is accurate enough. These people never could get above the level of domesticity; they were drowning in detergents. Or, when they were promoted, in Martinis.

I should know, for I tried to be one of them for a while. I didn't get far in that line—ruining the soul was not my forte. But it wasn't for want of trying. I got a job as an editor in a publishing house, and for five years I went to work every morning in an office in New York.

Why on earth? I think it was the craziest thing I ever did. But it didn't seem crazy at the time. In the first place, there was the exhaustion I have mentioned. In the second place, after the war when I and others like myself went forth into the world, we found an older generation who were really and truly void of ideas. These were people who had been out of work in the Depression, and now they had jobs and they were glad to be selling soap. The novels and movies of the times—*The Man in the Gray Flannel Suit*, etc.—show what they were like. If they were connected with the arts, book publishing for example, these men and women would sell books as though they were soap.

I was not experienced enough to know that this was not the way the world had to be, that there were other possibilities. Contrary to what many people think, especially in America where everyone flatters the young, idealism is not a characteristic of youth, but of experience. So I went to work for some soap salesmen who called themselves publishers.

Then I got married and moved to the suburbs, for this seemed to go along with the job.

Sometimes I am astonished how typical I have been. It is as though I have submitted myself to ordinary experiences deliberately, living as most people live, so that I could write poems about it. I wanted to write extraordinary poems about being ordinary—not as others do, ordinary poems about being extraordinary.

*

On the left side of the train the river broadened and the banks rose into low hills. Linked barges made their way on the stream at twilight, and sometimes I wished I were on a raft drifting somewhere. An American dream . . . but it had been done. At the station I got in my car and drove into the hills where lights were just beginning to shine. In the summer the valley was leafy, green and hot; in the fall the trees put on countless hues of red and yellow and an infinite melancholy; in winter you drove through the ghosts of trees and hills, and it was hard to believe that anyone lived behind the window where a light as sharp as ammonia needled your eyes.

I was living with my wife and child in a small apartment on a second floor in the middle of nowhere. All over America there are such lives, removed from the stir of cities, far away from smoke-filled rooms and the hum of voices. At the end of the driveway someone has retired from the world; his only connection with it is the plumbing, the electricity, the telephone. These identical fixtures are all that relate one house to another. And somewhere else, perhaps, at the moment someone else is listening to the same record. Oh yes, and television . . . now almost everybody has one, and at this moment ten million people are watching the Sid Caesar Show or the commercial about Suzy Spotless. And Paladin: "They whipped your father with barbed wire, and then they shot him like a sick steer."

We could study Italian. Some day we might go to Italy. How are you?—*Come sta?*

So-so—*Così così.*

Did you have a good time at the tea?—*Si e divertita al tè?*

To tell the truth I did not have such a good time.—*Per dir la verità non me sono divertita molto.*

My wife would go to bed—she had to be up early with the baby—and I would read late into the night, listening to the boughs rustling in the wind. "In the middle of my life's journey I found myself in a wood."

Sometimes I'd watch TV, anything that came on the screen. It would be two o'clock and I'd be watching the Late Late Show.

No strings and no connections,
No ties to my affections,
I'm fancy free
And free for anything fancy.

156

Fred in his top hat and Ginger in her riding habit join hands and dance in the band pavilion. What does it matter where the music comes from or that the plot is absurd—talk about Theatre of the Absurd!—for the tunes are wonderful. Then Fred appears on a stage with a backdrop of street lamps and the Eiffel Tower.

> O I'm putting on my top hat,
> Tying up my white tie,
> Brushing off my tails . . .

Then in a trice you fly from London to Venice, canals with banks of white tile like an enormous bathroom, and another melody begins.

> And I seem to find the happiness I seek
> When we're out together dancing cheek to cheek.

It was there I found the happiness I sought, down to the last drops of the *"Piccolino"*, when "Venetian sons and daughters"—the men with their bell-bottom trousers and broad hats looked more like Argentinian caballeros than Italians—were whirling together, and the lovers went off dancing.

XXIX

In the post-war years poets, like everyone else, seemed exhausted. Many poets were content to write in traditional forms, taking their ideas from the critics.

T. S. Eliot had said it was an age of criticism. He meant

the generation of 1910 when the Imagist movement started. The Imagists had original theories and wrote brilliant poems. Some of their attitudes were adopted by men who called themselves the New Critics. These men concentrated on "explication", that is, examining the "technique" of poems. They explicated the poems of Donne, but they no longer dealt with poetry as a vital, original force. They didn't ask fundamental questions—"Is this a poem?" "What is poetry?"—but knew how to explain symbols and discuss sentence structure.

Contrary to what critics said, after the Imagists there had actually been a dearth of criticism. The men who grew in the shadow of Eliot and Pound were content to follow in their footsteps, imitating their opinions and even their styles. In the 'thirties and 'forties poets tried to make themselves a career in the grand manner: they knew what it was to sound like a great poet, but they had not begun, as Yeats had, by walking the roads and finding a subject of his own, or like Eliot and Pound by meeting to discuss the meaning of images.

As a result, in the 'fifties there were no ideas about poetry that spoke to a young man who was just beginning. Frost and Stevens were writing poems, but they said nothing to the young, and the poets of the 'forties, men such as Delmore Schwartz and Karl Shapiro, were imitating their elders and had no theories about what they were doing. Consequently, those who came after them were wandering about in a desert in which there were no signposts. The epigones of the New Critics were still writing textual analyses of Donne, but these were of little use to young men who had been through the war and had seen a great deal and wished to express their feelings about the contemporary world. There was no nourishment to be had. We wanted bread and were given these stones.

The New Critics—R. P. Blackmur, Cleanth Brooks, John

Crowe Ransom, Allen Tate, Robert Penn Warren, and their men in the universities—regarded the poem as an object for rigorous, empirical, objective analysis (textual criticism). The poem was treated "primarily as poetry and not another thing", without reference to the author's life or intention (the intentional fallacy), to history, to genre, or to the effect of the work on the reader's feelings (the affective fallacy). Young poets hastened to oblige the critics by writing poems that would be suitable for this kind of analysis. Above all, personality was to be omitted, except under a mask, and the speaking voice was ironic. Discipline of this kind produced two brilliant poets: Robert Lowell (*Lord Weary's Castle*, 1946) and Richard Wilbur (*The Beautiful Changes*, 1947). They were like Browning and Tennyson. Lowell was full of obscure references; he wrote couplets or alternate rhymes that pounded like a jack-hammer; his subject was violence and guilt:

> Is there no way to cast my hook
> Out of this dynamited brook?

Wilbur wrote in elegant, mellifluous stanzas; his poems were a dance of similes and play of ideas:

> Mind in the purest play is like some bat
> That beats about in caverns all alone . . .

The technical skill of these poems was extraordinary, but when I did glimpse a meaning it was far removed from any life I had known. The poems of Lowell and Wilbur had been praised by the New Critics and noticed even by Eliot, so the fault must be in myself. Reviewers were vying to compare Lowell and Wilbur. One reviewer praised Wilbur's elegance and Lowell's passionate complexity. Another reviewer said that though Lowell was passionate he was also graceful, and though Wilbur was elegant this should not blind us to the intensity of his metaphysics. But when I read the poems they were not talking about anything that interested me.

Such understanding as I had of the New Critics came from talking to Christopher Green. Christopher had lived in Cambridge and attended writers' conferences at Kenyon College where he developed an English accent. He actually knew John Crowe Ransom, Allen Tate, and R. P. Blackmur. His poems had been anthologized by Oscar Williams. In other words, Christopher was promising, and his name would have been included in any list of the younger poets of the time. I admired Christopher's poetry, though I did not wish to write like this myself. The following lines are taken from his poem, "Low Tide on Martha's Vineyard".

In Back Bay, where a street
Grows narrower, my Grandaunt Abigail
Is reading tea-leaves, and the scuds★ are pale.
But Uncle Matt stays in his room
In tennis shoes, still wearing the costume
He wore with Dewey in Manila's bay.
"Beans!" we can hear him shout. "Beans every day?"
We are pretending that we haven't heard,
While strangers wink and whisper, "Mum's the word."

"Low Tide" had been admired and anthologized, and none other than L. K. Piknitt had written an explication:

The employment of the "scuds" is—let us not be chary of praise—a stroke of talent, and if it be considered that "beans" follows soon after, the employment verges on genius. The words are in origin and have remained in usage both light. One comes from a word meaning to stir to the side, and the other is derived from Anglo-Saxon. Whether the history of the words was present in Mr. Green's mind when he chose them is immaterial;

★ The Back Bay term, but not universal. In Cambridge they are called "scutts" (C.G.).

160

the pristine flavor is still active by tradition and is what gives rare taste to the lines—"scuds" evidencing the peripheral, "pushed-to-the-side" quality of Abigail's life in Back Bay, "beans" reminding us of another, more vigorous, ruder tradition. On the strength of such usages alone, I do not hesitate to predict for Christopher Green an *oeuvre* in verse no less realized than that of Robert Lowell.

It was Christopher who gave me my first opportunity to meet a really famous poet, Dylan Thomas. Chris said, "I'm having a party for Dylan." He hesitated a moment, then said, "You can come if you like."

I turned up on the dot at the apartment of Christopher's parents on Park Avenue. I was the first to arrive. Christopher's mother was a cultured lady who, like her son, had an English accent. I put down my glass on a table and she hastened to slide something between the glass and the surface. I spoke to Chris's father for a few minutes. He was in business downtown and seemed, in comparison with his wife and son, rather subdued. The other guests arrived, and then Dylan Thomas himself, surrounded by several people who moved in front of him and to the side. I was surprised at Thomas's appearance. I had been expecting a slender man with a faun-face, like the photographs in anthologies. Instead there was a middle-aged man with a pudgy face who sat down heavily and said nothing. Someone told me he had just come back from California, so I walked over and asked him how he had liked it there. He stared at me with glazed eyes, then he belched. This was the extent of my conversation with Dylan Thomas. I regret the lost opportunity, for so many other people have stories about their evenings with him and the brilliance of his talk. I have never been fortunate in my meetings with great men.

When I left the apartment Christopher's mother and

father were standing by the door. I said, "Thank you," and added, "You must be very proud of Christopher." "Oh, we are," said Mrs. Green, though with a rather stern expression as though reproving me for having any doubts about the matter.

The curious thing about Christopher was that though he moved in literary circles and wrote such elegant verse, there was another side of his life that was completely different and involved him in all sorts of difficulties, yet he never wrote poems about it. He was lecherous and very attractive to women.

I met him on Madison Avenue one afternoon in the company of a stunningly good-looking girl of about nineteen named Jill. She had the high cheekbones, straight nose and blond hair of a fashion model, and this, it turned out, was her profession. We had a drink in a cocktail lounge. Christopher had met her only a few weeks ago and, to my astonishment, he said they were getting married. What on earth did she expect to find in him? She looked like the destined companion of South American millionaires. But apparently she was tired of all that, and wanted nothing better than to read poems and literary criticism for the rest of her life. She told hair-raising stories about her life as a model in the garment district: "The men are always trying to feel you up, and the women too." But it seemed that she had moved through all this unharmed. Perhaps it was the result of her religious training. Until she was sixteen she had been in a convent. The more she revealed about herself, the more trouble I had making the pieces fit.

At this time I had separated from my wife. Our marriage had not been a success. I was living in furnished rooms again, and finding it hard to make ends meet. So when Jill asked me to come with Chris for a home-cooked dinner I accepted with alacrity.

Jill shared the apartment with another model, who was

getting ready to leave when we arrived. She was in her underwear and finished dressing in front of us. I thought this was strange and blamed myself for thinking so. After all, in modelling circles they were always taking off their clothes in public.

Later that evening more of Jill's friends came, till we were having a party. At one point Jill dissolved in tears and there was a huddle of women in that corner. One of them told me later in confidence that Jill was terrified.

"Of what?"

"Christopher."

"Why? He's perfectly harmless."

"It's not just him, it could be any man. You see, she's a virgin. She's never known any man, really. She's terrified of getting married."

Another woman who had been talking to Jill confirmed this account, and we agreed that it was a frightening situation for Jill, and wondered if Christopher would be able to handle such a delicate problem.

Christopher and Jill were duly married and I attended the wedding reception at his parents' apartment. Jill's side of the ceremony was represented by three or four of her girl friends, also models, for it seemed that all her relatives had been absented by illnesses or deaths. The wedding reception, with all these beautiful models moving through it, was like a Hollywood scene. The talk was very high-toned, all about where Jill and Chris were going to spend their summer, on the Cape. Mrs. Green passed around the room and wherever she had been people seemed to have been converted immediately into white Anglo-Saxon Protestants, and most of them into Episcopalians. Hauteur was rife. Mrs. Green told me that her new daughter-in-law had an interesting background; her family were old French Huguenots.

Going down the elevator, however, with the girl I had

brought, a tough cookie who worked as a reporter, she whispered, "I've got to tell you something." I restrained her until we were out in the street, when she said, "I was listening to a couple of Jill's friends. My God, they're all call-girls." I told her not to be silly. At that moment I was feeling Waspish myself, inhaling the good sea air of the Cape, touching the clean brown sand, a world in which the nicest, most beautiful people got married and wrote poems and lived happily ever after.

If I were writing a novel I would make thirty chapters out of what the reader has already guessed: that Jill was a liar and far from inexperienced. The "convent" she attended was actually a home for wayward girls. I would show her, a few weeks after the marriage, taking up her old habits again. I would tell how, the more she deceived Chris, the more infatuated he became. Once she ran away with a Portuguese fisherman. Finally, with the luck that seems to pursue such women in our time as sorrow pursued their unfortunate sisters in the nineteenth century, she left Chris for an Italian count who had, believe it or not, a fortune in Brazilian investments. Now Jill is a *bona fide* countess living in a palace on the outskirts of Florence.

Chris must have suffered a great deal. Indeed, I know that he did, for though he was only thirty his hair began to turn grey and his brow grew lined. Yet none of his feelings were expressed in his poetry so that you could recognize them. They were hidden in symbols and distorted by irony. Once I dared to hint at this and he said, "You're wrong, absolutely wrong. I've written it all in a poem." He showed me the poem, a verse play on the theme of Andromeda: "The Scene: Ethiopia, the sea shore, near a great rock." As the play opened, Perseus—who had once come flying to save Andromeda from the sea monster—was once again paying a visit to Ethiopia. He had been neglecting Andromeda for years and now he said that he was getting married to another woman. If I rember rightly, Andromeda put an end to that by carving him up. The whole thing was in rhymed couplets. I wrote down the final speech by Andromeda; it struck me at the time as immensely moving.

> How still and soft it is, the twilight hour.
> I feel the soothing, melancholy power
> Of passing time. For princesses have gone
> And still the tranquil waves come tiding on.
> My life was like the trouble that a star
> Casts in a dream, mysterious and far.
> But I am living—in my life I wake
> And find myself once more chained to the stake.
> What's night to all the world is noon to me,
> And from the surface of the moonlit sea
> Monsters and nightmares in disorder rise,
> Poseidon with his beard and angry eyes,
> My father's hands, the corpse of Perseus,
> And love, the monster that devours us.
> This is the end, Andromeda remains
> On the dark rock, in her immortal chains.

What on earth did this have to do with Christopher's marriage? Was Jill "Andromeda"? Had Chris seen himself in the role of Perseus coming to the rescue of a model in the garment district? Or was this a variation of the "Albertine gambit", a transposition of sexes, so that he himself was Andromeda, and Jill, who in fact had been the one to take flight, Perseus? It is all confused and pointless, and I have the impression from this poem and other writings of the time in which legends and myths were used, that there were not men living in those days, not even poets, but masks, *personae*, aspects of the New Criticism.

XXX

It may be true, as Nick says in *Gatsby*, that the world is best looked at from a single window, but the writer's life is a very narrow window.

Writers are not the best company, they are too full of themselves; nor are they even good conversationalists, for they are preoccupied with the ideas they will be able to use. And among writers, poets are the least interesting company of all, for they are usually daydreaming. Yet I have found myself over and over again in the company of writers and especially poets, simply because I was a writer, when I would much rather have been somewhere else. It's too bad that the love of books brings you into contact with the people who write them.

In America it is common for a writer, after his first book, to have nothing more to say, because he has had no new experiences of any importance and has just hung around with other writers. By importance I mean emotional and intellectual content. In this fix the writer is likely to look for adventures, go to the Brazilian jungle, become interested in science or politics, travel around with a candidate for the presidency, but these activities—the "real world" that magazines commission writers to write articles about—have no connection with his own individual artistic character. So he is trapped in a career, and his life is not different from the professional life of lawyers, actors or baseball players. The man is distorted by the profession.

Looking back, the people I have known best have been writers. With the exception of women. But they would require another book and I am not prepared to write it. As

Tolstoy said, I will tell what I think about women when my coffin is open and I can jump in and slam it shut.

So for the present I shall continue to talk about writing. It is a narrow window, but as wide as others.

★

In the early 1950s poetry was at a low ebb. The best-known younger poets—men such as Christopher Green—were the products of universities and writers' conferences. They published in established literary magazines, *The Hudson Review* and so on, and were awarded prizes and fellowships. When I had spent any time in the company of such people I found myself depressed; there was nothing to talk about, only mild gossip punctuated with the eternal question, "Have you read?"—meaning some new volume of verse or a critical article. These people had no subject, least of all themselves. Their existence seemed real only when their name appeared in print, most real when it was in an anthology with the date of birth next to it and a blank for the date of death. You felt that they could hardly wait for the terminal date to be filled in.

My dissatisfaction with the literary world began to be acute. For some time I had been publishing poems in the quarterlies, and had a contract with *The New Yorker* stipulating that I was to let them have the first look at anything I wrote. My poems came out in *The New Yorker*, and if a large public means anything—and some people think it does—then I should have been satisfied. But, to the contrary, when I saw one of my poems in thin type next to the ads for shirts and whisky and sports cars, I was depressed. I was sure that no one would read the poem, or if they did, anything intelligent that it might say would be immediately overwhelmed by the fatuous thoughts rising out of the advertisements.

Moreover, the close-editing policy of *The New Yorker* was annoying. They queried every fact and were always recommending changes for the better. This might be tolerable in prose—though some fiction writers found it less and less tolerable—but in poetry it was ludicrous. On one occasion I sent them a poem that mentioned the Conquistadors in the lines,

> And murdering, in a religious way,
> Brings Jesus to the Gulf of Mexico.

I got back a three-page single-spaced letter from the editors, apparently the result of research and consultation, informing me that Jesus had never gone to the Gulf of Mexico. But Cortez had, and as his name contained the same number of syllables, the meter wouldn't be upset if I said Cortez instead of Jesus. What irritated me about this was not so much the censorship as the hypocrisy: why couldn't they just say they didn't want any mention of Jesus, good or bad? I came to understand their editorial policy—any writing that might really disturb anyone was out. Over the magazine there hung a tiresome air of facetiousness; at the same time there was a pretence of being serious. Stories about the neuroses of well-to-do people living in the suburbs were acceptable and they printed them all the time, for these of course disturbed no one, they were just more of the pseudo self-criticism the middle class indulges in, that enables them to think that they are thinking.

The New Yorker put great stress on the checking of facts, and the finished story or poem presented an entirely smooth, impenetrable surface. In one poem I mentioned a well-known photograph by Matthew Brady, depicting a dead Confederate soldier in the Devil's Den at Gettysburg. They wanted to know the number of the plate in the Brady collection. On another occasion I referred to a place named Beaulieu and an Irishman who had lived there. They wanted me to clarify this; Bealieu, they told me was in England, not far from Stonehenge. The Irishman, of course, would be Yeats. Would I explain exactly what I intended to imply by all this? I wrote back that my Beaulieu was in France on the Mediterranean, and the Irishman I had in mind was more like Scott Fitzgerald. In a return letter they suggested that I would find Yeats better suited to my purpose.

I have tried to imagine what it would have been like if Coleridge had submitted "Kubla Khan" to *The New Yorker*.

> In Xanadu did Kubla Khan
> A stately pleasure-dome decree:
> Where Alph, the sacred river, ran
> Through caverns measureless to man
>   Down to a sunless sea.
> So twice five miles of fertile ground
> With walls and towers were girdled round:
> And there were gardens bright with sinuous rills,
> Where blossomed many an incense-bearing tree;
> And here were forests ancient as the hills,
> Enfolding sunny spots of greenery . . .

The New Yorker might have written to Coleridge as follows.

Dear Sam:

We liked "Kubla Khan" very much and want to take it. Our readers, however, have some queries that we hope you can clear up.

"*Xanadu.*" One of our readers points out that this name is unfamiliar to the general reader, and that the poem would get off to a much better start if you simply said China. You would lose a syllable this way, but you could keep the meter if you added another word. For example:
> In China once did Kubla Khan . . .

"*pleasure-dome.*" We don't visualize this clearly. Do

you mean hanging gardens, as in Babylon, or are you maybe thinking of the Crystal Palace Exhibition?

"*Alph . . . Down to a sunless sea.*" This presents a real problem. If the caverns are, as you say, "measureless to man", how can we know that the sea is "sunless"? No one will ever have seen it. I hate to be Johnsonian about this, but some of our readers are sure to pick it up.

"*twice five miles.*" This seems rather unnecessarily specific and also long-winded. If you must, couldn't you just say "ten"?

Best wishes,
Gerald

★

I was invited to a party being held by the editors of a new literary magazine. Arriving at an address on the East Side I found myself among the most successful first-novelists of the time. Their first novels had been handled by leading literary agents and acclaimed at length in such places as *Time* and *The New York Times*. Their conversation was all about agents and reviews. They seemed not at all interested in ideas, not even in writing novels, but only in plays they had seen and houses they were renting for the summer. They were what would be called a few years later "the beautiful people". Listening to them I was filled with the kind of despair I felt when I read a poem in *The New Yorker*. I had a feeling of panic and broke out in a cold sweat. I went for my overcoat and plunged out through the door just as the main party was arriving, more first-novelists with their wives. I got on a bus going down Fifth Avenue, and remember thinking, That's finished. If that's what it takes to be an up-and-coming writer in New York, I'll never make it.

Everyone seemed to be at loose ends. One day Ginsberg

came to see me at the publishing house. He showed me a few poems in free verse—flat, feeble little things—and said he had been reading William Carlos Williams. We had little to say to each other. He said he was going away to Mexico. I watched him leave and turned back to reading another manuscript.

At this time, luckily, I met one man from whom I could learn something. This was Saul Bellow. He himself was a product of literary milieux, and had written for *The Partisan Review* and that gang. His early novels, tightly constructed and limited in their objectives, had pleased the critics. His future seemed assured if only he were willing to take one step at a time. The people who keep an eye on such things are not averse to helping young writers if they progress in an agreeable manner—that is, according to the rules. It is necessary at every step for the young novelist to approach his elders, who are presumably his betters, and to enlist their help and advice. But Bellow suddenly took a giant step. He had discovered his subject: being a Jew in America—not the Jew trying to be an American but the American Jew learning to be himself—and in *The Adventures of Augie March* he wrote an expansive, eccentric novel about such a man. Moreover, it was not a New York novel, it was situated in Chicago. Some of the critics thought he had gone too far, but when the reports started coming in and it was evident that *Augie* was a band-wagon, they hastened to get on it. In spite of their praise, and though *Augie* was not the masterpiece they then said it was—for it was too long and rambling and the boisterousness of the main character often rang false—nevertheless Bellow had done something new. In fact he had created a *genre* of fiction that would in the coming decade be practised by other "Jewish" writers, Malamud and Roth being the most successful.

I was visiting friends in the Village when Bellow came in, carrying a briefcase. His overcoat was sprinkled with snow;

he had been giving a talk at the New School for Social Research, and had come through a snow storm. It is a strange thing about the New School, you always get snowed or rained upon, the nights you teach there. But it wasn't the weather that was bothering Bellow, it was a man who had followed him up the street after his lecture to tell him he didn't know anything about novels really, for he was only a novelist. Finally, in order to get rid of this example of a critic, Bellow had swung at him in self-defence with his briefcase. He hadn't connected, but he was still dishevelled and excited. He felt this was a symbolic encounter, everything he was trying to accomplish being threatened by a fool. He was exhilarated; there is nothing like opposition, driving a man against the wall, to make him believe in the reality of his ideas.

Over the next three years I got to know Bellow, but here I must mention a curious thing. There were many people who knew him, and each had a different idea of the man. One saw him as a tough guy; another saw him as *ein mensch*, sympathetic and full of wisdom. For my part, I saw Bellow as a man who had a magnificent original prose style and who, moreover, had fared ahead of me in a world of marital troubles, alimony payments, visiting hours—the whole tangled, perplexing world of divorce that I myself, along with many other Americans, had begun to explore.

Divorce was the last frontier of an American turning toward suburbia. Paying alimony was the middle-class American's substitute for cutting his throat. Visiting hours were his equivalent for purgatory. Bellow was going through them all with expressions of grief and rage, but he survived and, moreover, had hitched up with a new wife who was young and devoted to him, who stood by his side at the helm on those rough seas where the next wave, a telephone call from "her" lawyer demanding more money, would crash on the deck and nearly swamp the boat. But they steered through, and Bellow continued to write, planning novels, plays, stories, and writing reviews besides. His study was a welter of books and long sheets of paper piled on a table. He complained about being distracted. He had an idea that not only business people but also people who asked you to write reviews and the people who ran universities were engaged in a kind of conspiracy to stop you writing. Not to mention lawyers and ex-wives. It was poetry they were all against. They were all trying to distract you from writing poetry. By which, of course, he meant prose, and indeed I thought his prose was more poetic than the verse of the poets I knew.

One day at Tivoli he showed me pages of a short novel he was finishing. I sat on the lawn reading after he had gone back into the house. As I read time was suspended, and when I came to the end I had a feeling I have had only two or three times in my life—that I was witnessing at first hand the creation of a masterpiece. The man who'd first seen the manuscript of a story by Gogol or Dostoevsky might have had the same feeling.

He, alone of all the people in the chapel, was sobbing. No one knew who he was.

One woman said, "Is that perhaps the cousin from New Orleans they were expecting?"

"It must be somebody real close to carry on so."

"Oh my, oh my! To be mourned like that," said one man and looked at Wilhelm's heavy shaken shoulders, his clutched face and whitened fair hair, with wide, glinting, jealous eyes.

"The man's brother, maybe?"

"Oh, I doubt that very much," said another bystander. "They're not alike at all. Night and day."

The flowers and lights fused ecstatically in Wilhelm's blind, wet eyes; the heavy sea-like music came up to his ears. It poured into him where he had hidden himself in the center of a crowd by the great and happy oblivion of tears. He heard it and sank deeper than sorrow, through torn sobs and cries toward the consummation of his heart's ultimate need.

I ran into the house with the manuscript and told Bellow, "It's great. And the part where Tommy is in the phone booth . . ."

He smiled and had a cunning look in his eyes. As with all first-rate writers at the height of their power, he knew very well what he had done.

I showed Saul a bunch of my poems. He said nothing about the poems that had been published by *The New Yorker*, *The Hudson Review*, and *The Paris Review*, but put his finger on a few lines, a fragment I did not understand myself.

> Though mad Columbus follows the sun
> Into the sea, we cannot follow.
> We must remain, to serve the returning sun,
> And to set tables for death . . .

"I like this," he said. "It shows a direction."

What the direction was, he did not say. But I often returned to look at the fragment, and years later when I began writing poems that meant something to me and had some of the same quality, I thought he had been astonishingly perceptive.

XXXI

I had come to know Donald Hall, who was editing poetry for *The Paris Review*. He accepted some of my poems with enthusiasm, and his suggestions were valuable. Soon we were friends, and have been friends for twenty years.

Sustained friendship among writers is not a common thing. They become resentful of criticism and think that the other person is trying to do them in, or they become jealous of his success. And then there are writers' affairs and marriages. It is hard for a woman to think that somebody else has known her husband before she has, and been friendly with her husband's other girls. She starts making snide remarks when the friend comes round. She points out that the old buddy is a bad influence—he is trying to stop John from working seriously, because he himself is burnt out. For years, as a matter of fact, it's been a one-way relationship, the weak leaning on the strong. Now that John is starting a new life it's time to get rid of the parasites.

Also, of course, we want things to stay as they are. We'd like our friends to keep on doing the things they were doing when we first knew them. We are likely to think that they did those things because we knew them. Yeats says:

We are never satisfied with the maturity of those whom we have admired in boyhood; and because we have seen their whole circle—even the most successful life is but a segment—we remain to the end their hardest critics. One old schoolfellow of mine will never believe that I have fulfilled the promise of some rough unscannable verses that I wrote before I was eighteen. Does any imaginative man find in maturity the admiration that his first half-articulate years aroused in some little circle; and is not the first success the greatest?

Donald and I were approached by Robert Pack, who had a project. He wanted to put out an anthology of poets under forty, and he had a publisher and the necessary financial backing. We agreed that we would edit the anthology together, and set about reading books and magazines. We met at Donald's house near Boston for our discussions or at my apartment on Riverside Drive. It seemed a simple matter to make such a collection. Donald was well read in contemporary English poetry—half the anthology was given to this—and all three of us thought we knew American poetry. Robert Frost wrote the introduction, and *The New Poets of England and America* was published.

Without intending to, we had created a furor. I had never imagined that an anthology could be taken so seriously, but this one was. In the first place it was regarded as an attempt to be definitive. But we had not intended to imply that these were the only poets in England and America. We were trying to make a representative selection, in so far as we were able. Now I can see that we were naïve. For years there had not been an important collection of contemporary poets, and so the book would be regarded as definitive.

Reviewers ignored the fact that, for practical reasons, poets over forty had been excluded, and they complained about the omission of older figures. And, of course, younger poets who had not been included were filled with rage. Some of these had published in such obscure places that they were virtually unknown, and I do not see how we could be blamed for not knowing their work. A little more research might have discovered Robert Duncan's early work, but Allen Ginsberg, for example, had not yet published "Howl".

Yet in the following years it was widely assumed that

we had read and excluded works such as "Howl". It has become, in fact, an accepted part of literary history that *The New Poets* was published according to certain literary prejudices that did not make room for the writing of the Beats, the Black Mountain poets, and other experimental writers. My observation of this error at first hand has left me suspicious of all histories of literary movements.

Having tried to set the record straight, I must add that, though the criticism of our motives was mistaken, much of the cricitism of the anthology was justified. It is true that it did not represent experimental verse sufficiently. This was certainly the fault of the editors, who leaned toward traditional ways of writing. This limitation of the anthology became more apparent as time went by, and people got in the habit of thinking of American poetry as divided in two groups: "academic" verse, represented by this anthology, and "non-academic" verse, represented by an anthology published a few years later, *The New American Poetry, 1945–1960*. Moreover, the editors of the first anthology taught for a living, and so did many of the poets. (Later on, some of the poets in *The New American Poetry*, also, would find employment in universities, but at this time they were claiming to be independent.) To the journalistic mind, with its fear of schoolmasters, the fact that some of the "New Poets of England and America" taught for a living was a handy peg on which to hang the label "academic".

But perhaps I had better go back to the beginning of the post-war period and trace the development of poetry up to the late 1950s, for a great deal was happening in these years.

★

In the 1940s three reputations overshadowed the writing of verse in America: W. B. Yeats, T. S. Eliot, W. H. Auden. Each spoke for an era: Yeats for romanticism and symbolism;

Eliot for the Imagist movement and then a turning toward dogma (for Eliot it was Christian dogma, for others Marxism); Auden for technical ingenuity and an agile curiosity turning in several directions—Marx, Freud, Kierkegaard, Christianity. Through the 1940s it was Auden who still influenced younger poets most clearly; in retrospect the poets of the time—Delmore Schwartz and Karl Shapiro come to mind—were imitating Auden more than they knew, together with imitations of Eliot and Yeats, and sometimes of Rilke. (It is odd to think of Rilke as a model in those years, for in his self-searching and his belief in "angels" Rilke was far removed from Marxist determinism and fashionable references to psychoanalysis.)

At the beginning of the 1950s Dylan Thomas burst on the American scene, bringing with him a new concept—at least it seemed new at the time—of poetry as the spoken rather than the written word. This example was to have a powerful effect some years later when the Beats and other poets began performing in public. This is anticipating, however, for in his poems Dylan Thomas was working in the old symbolist techniques; there was nothing in his concept of the poem itself that was new, only in the manner of delivery. When Thomas read aloud, poetry again became one of the performing arts.

From the end of the war until the mid-1950s there was a dearth of new ideas about poetry in America. Older poets—Robert Frost, Wallace Stevens, E. E. Cummings, Marianne Moore, William Carlos Williams, and Ezra Pound—were writing, but Pound, "*Il miglior fabbro*", was a patient in St. Elizabeth's Hospital, and the others, however fine their works might be, did not strike the young as teachers. Each older poet would come out of obscurity to be given a prize and have his vogue. So it was with Stevens after 1954 when the *Collected Poems* won the National Book Award. But the older poets were distant planets, each whirling in a separate volume. The influential ideas about poetry came from the New Critics and in the post-war years there was seen a phenomenon, poetry imitating criticism.

I have spoken of the effect of the New Critics, their emphasis on textual analysis with the consequence that poetry that lent itself to textual analysis was deemed superior. The more rhetorical complexity, the better. The more tension, irony, and so on, the more subtle and remote the relationship of the poet to the poem, the more the poem seemed detached from its maker—the more, in short, the poem seemed a construction cut off from history and personality, the better. Among the younger poets, Lowell and Wilbur had produced the finest examples of poetry rising out of the New Criticism. Most of the poetry published in quarterlies was of this kind.

And when we put together *The New Poets of England and America* this was the kind of poetry we found. The anthology presented a number of poets who had much in common with Lowell and Wilbur. W. S. Merwin, Anthony Hecht, Howard Nemerov—in different tones each was producing a kind of verse that was guarded, indirect, self-deprecatory, and usually written in rhymed stanzas. Perhaps the most representative poet in the anthology was Howard Nemerov, who wrote of a vacuum cleaner:

> The house is so quiet now
> The vacuum cleaner sulks in the corner closet,
> Its bag limp as a stopped lung, its mouth
> Grinning into the floor, maybe at my
> Slovenly life, my dog-dead youth . . .

Such poetry was too domestic. However, something new might be observed in the poems by W. D. Snodgrass we printed in the anthology, later included in his first book, *Heart's Needle*. Though he wrote in chiselled stanzas,

Snodgrass's style was intimate. The subject was divorce and visiting hours.

> If I loved you, they said, I'd leave
>   and find my own affairs.
> Well, once again this April, we've
>   come around to the bears;
> punished and cared for, behind bars,
>   the coons on bread and water
> stretch thin black fingers after ours.
>   And you are still my daughter.

This signalled a change toward a more direct kind of writing, and the change was coming from other directions at the same time. Let us step back to Pound, doing penance in St. Elizabeth's. Pound had been the most useful disseminator of ideas about writing in English in this century, but Pound's poems had no influence while the New Criticism predominated. The "open", discursive writing of the *Cantos* did not please the taste nurtured on Yeats, Eliot, and Auden. These men were "makers" of finished poems; Pound was a bard, a prophet, and his poems were never finished. W. C. Williams, with his flat, prosey lines and "American speech rhythms", did not excite readers accustomed to the regular accents of Yeats, Eliot's music, and Auden's jazzy stanzas. But an underground of new poets had been springing up, who took Pound and Williams as masters. These poets—Charles Olson, Robert Duncan, Robert Creeley, Denise Levertov—developed a school of "Projective Verse". According to Olson, their theorist, Projective Verse was to be "composition by field". He defined a basis for structure of the poem in terms of its *kinetics*—"the poem itself must, at all points, be a high-energy-construct and, at all points, an energy discharge". Form, said Olson, is never more than an extension of content, and "One perception must immediately and directly lead to a further perception". He distinguished between breathing and hearing, as these relate to the line: "The line comes (I swear it) from the breath, from the breathing of the man who writes, at that moment that he writes."

The poems of Olson's followers were harvested in the anthology *The New American Poetry*, published in 1960. Several of these poets were Westerners, and perhaps the most outstanding, Robert Duncan and Gary Snyder, wrote of Oregon and California—unlike the poets of the 1957 anthology who were attached to the East Coast. The "New American" poets wrote lines according to Olson's system of breathing (I find Olson's theories hard to explain, as I am sure he must have found them himself). These poets were rhapsodic; at times they seemed, as has been said of Pound, to be translating at sight from an unknown poem. For example, in "A Poem Beginning with a Line by Pindar," Duncan wrote:

The Thundermakers Descend

damerging a nuv. A nerb.
The present dented of the U
nighted stayd. States. The heavy clod?
Cloud. Invades the brain. What
if lilacs last in *this* dooryard bloomd?

Gary Snyder was best when he detailed his logging-camp and hiking experiences.

Stone-flake and salmon.
The pure, sweet, straight-splitting
with a ping
Red cedar of the thick coast valleys
Shake-blanks on the mashed ferns
the charred logs . . .

Another group of new poets was represented in the 1960 anthology—the Beats (from "beat up" or "beatific"—no one knows what the word means exactly, probably a little of both). The most notable of the Beats was Allen Ginsberg, whose debt was to Williams rather than Pound. Listing common things in the American grain, he wrote about supermarkets and bus terminals. Ginsberg's long loose lines were not in the manner of Williams, who was always tightly controlled; in rhythm the model was Whitman. What was original, however, was Ginsberg's temperament; he had a talent for hysteria. He spoke or rather ululated for the middle-class children who had grown up after World War II in an affluent society and who suffered from acute neuroses. The Beats were creating a subculture with their own heroes and saints—smokers of marijuana, motor-cyclists and jazz musicians who spoke familiarly of Buddha:

> I saw the best minds of my generation destroyed by madness, starving hysterical naked,
> dragging themselves through the negro streets at dawn looking for an angry fix,
> angelheaded hipsters burning for the ancient heavenly connection to the starry dynamo in the machinery of night . . .

With Snodgrass's *Heart's Needle*, the poems of Duncan and Snyder, and Ginsberg's "Howl"—though they arrived from different directions, Snodgrass from the New Criticism, Duncan and Snyder from the ideas of Pound and Williams as interpreted by Olson, and Ginsberg from bohemia, with some credit to Williams—we begin to see an idea held in common, a turning away from the New Critics' idea of the poem-as-object, a construction, and a turning toward poetry of direct personal utterance. Irony was being replaced by sincerity. Lowell took the step in 1959 with *Life Studies*; with his defection from the teachings of Brooks and

Warren one could see the handwriting on the wall. The new sincerity produced, in the manner of Lowell, so-called "confessional" verse—Anne Sexton (*To Bedlam and Part Way Back*) and Sylvia Plath (*Ariel*)—and in the coffee-houses an outpouring of monologues in the manner of Ginsberg.

4

XXXII

One day, without having given the matter much thought, I left publishing forever. I simply walked out. I would probably have been fired anyway, as the publishers were preparing to dispense with editors altogether. They had found a new system which seemed to work much better than reading manuscripts and deciding whether or not to publish them. They would simply send a manuscript to one of the book clubs that distributed thousands of books. If the club said they would accept the book for their list, then our house would publish it. In this way the house could do without editors and be sure of sales.

In any case, I had come to realize that I would never be a successful editor. Most of the books we published I thought were rubbish, and the attitude showed in my dealings with their authors. Besides, this kind of editing was being replaced by another for which I had no talent whatsoever—the ability to think up a book and find someone who would write it. Increasingly publishers had to create new markets, and in order to do so they must find new authors; and if they could not find them, authors must be created.

But how would I earn a living? There was only one congenial possibility—to teach. It was true that teaching did not pay, but neither had editing. People said that teaching was bad for a writer, it was a sheltered world. I recalled a remark in *Time Magazine* about poets "wrapped in the cocoon of teaching". But I knew some of the people who worked on *Time* and could not imagine a more unreal life than that. At least in teaching you would be likely to be dealing with material that was valuable, and at the end of the day you would not feel that you would have to get drunk. No, these common objections to teaching did not strike me as important; besides, everyone is a different case, and the atmosphere of a university that makes so many American writers uneasy has never troubled me. Perhaps this is because I don't expect the university to provide me with spiritual nourishment. And I don't mix writing and teaching—I work at one or the other. No one can stand the man who feels that teaching is keeping him from writing, or the man who writes like a teacher.

Some people in universities expect to be promoted for writing poems, novels, or plays. I wanted no part of this. Writing was something I did for my own satisfaction, and I didn't want a committee to feel that they had a right to go sniffing around it. Moreover, I did not want to have to teach "creative writing", as most writers in universities who do not have a degree find themselves compelled to.

Once upon a time the making of poetry was taught, in Scotland, Ireland and Wales. People then were as serious about poetry as they are these days about politics and business. The teaching was by poets, and the curriculum was in three parts: memorizing, composing, and criticizing. Each pupil had his own separate cubicle where he memorized poems and stories assigned by his instructor. He lay on his back in order to compose, with the curtains drawn to exclude daylight. In the evenings the pupils recited what they had learned and written.

The bardic schools were very different from our "creative writing workshops". At best, writing courses give lonely people some company. But the atmosphere is all wrong; the students are hoping to get credit for their writing toward a degree, and the instructors are compelled to encourage them to write, even if they have no talent. How can poetry come of this? Young writers would be better off in a bar, or in love, or at sea. Universities are one thing, and life and poetry another.

I would get the Ph.D. that you had to have in order to teach literature and I would teach just that, and writing would be for my own pleasure.

★

I found myself once more at Columbia, registering for courses and going to classes. I was quite happy to be a graduate student. I had fallen in with others who were returning to the university after experiences like my own, and we felt that we were on a holiday. We did not expect the university to change our lives; we knew what we wanted to do, and this was just a place that could equip us with the skill.

Perhaps because we were older we were struck by the comical side of things. There was Saul Galin, for example. Saul had grown up in a tough neighbourhood, the East Bronx. Some of the boys he had known were now in the rackets or in jail. If this had been the 'sixties, Saul might have been a campus revolutionary—the present generation has been admirable in refusing to put up with academic nonsense. But as this was 1955 he submitted, as we all did, to the usual "requirements". When it came to choosing a thesis topic, the only topic that was acceptable to Saul's committee was a study of the Georgian poets, and Saul, who had grown up between a candy store and a kosher butcher's, set himself to collecting information about Englishmen who had written poems about birds and flowers. When Saul went through the defence of his thesis, his innate loathing of nature and all her works, of Masefield, Davies, Hodgson and the other songsters of the English counties, could not fail to be apparent. At one point he let slip the fact that he really didn't give a damn about birds.

189

The rest of his defence was difficult, one examiner in particular taking it upon himself to ask searching questions. Saul was passed, however. Then he discovered the reason for this particular examiner's hostility; he was a member of the Audubon Society and had taken Saul's contempt for birds as a personal affront.

★

One day Allen Ginsberg came back to Columbia. I had heard that he had written a long poem that he read to big audiences in San Francisco. The account of the performance was like Mark Twain's description of the Royal Nonesuch:

> . . . when he'd got everybody's expectations up high enough, he rolled up the curtain, and the next minute the king come a-prancing out on all fours, naked; and he was painted all over, ring-streaked-and-striped, all sorts of colours, as splendid as a rainbow. And—but never mind the rest of his outfit; it was just wild, but it was awful funny.

The next I knew, Ginsberg was in New York. I heard that he was going around the publishing houses carrying his own writings and those of his friends, Kerouac and so on, walking right into publishers' offices and telling them they had to publish these things. The ladies at *Mademoiselle* had been very taken with him.

Then, in the manner of a Greek play where the messengers come running in, one of my fellow instructors came up to the apartment where I was correcting papers, to tell me that Ginsberg had been looking for me. He had walked down the corridor in Hamilton Hall, throwing open the doors and shouting, "Where's Louis Simpson? Honour the poet!" With a friend like this, who needed an enemy? I had been trying my best to remove the impression in the

English Department that I wrote poems. Over there they didn't like poetry, and though they wrote articles on Keats and Wordsworth they would never have allowed them to teach there.

I had bought a copy of Allen's "Howl", an odd, black little book, and now I sat down to read it. I thought it was hysterical. And what was this? Ginsberg had a nerve, putting me in his creepy poem!

> Who threw their watches off the roof to cast their ballot for Eternity outside of Time, & alarm clocks fell on their heads every day for the next decade . . .

From thought to action was only a moment. I sat down and wrote a parody.

SQUEAL

I saw the best minds of my generation
Destroyed—Marvin
Who spat out poems; Potrzebie
Who coagulated a new bop literature in fifteen
Novels; Alvin
Who in his as yet unwritten autobiography
Gave Brooklyn an original *lex loci*.
They came from all over, from the pool room,
The bargain basement, the rod,
From Whitman, from Parkersburg, from Rimbaud
New Mexico, but mostly
They came from colleges, ejected
For drawing obscene diagrams of the Future.

They came here to L.A.,
Flexing their members, growing hair,
Planning immense unlimited poems,
More novels, more poems, more autobiographies.

It's love I'm talking about, you dirty bastards!

191

Love in the bushes, love in the freight car!
I saw them fornicating and being fornicated,
Saying to Hell with you!

America.
America is full of Babbitts.
America is run by money.

What was it Walt said? Go West!
But the important thing is the return ticket.
The road to publicity runs by Monterey.
I saw the best minds of my generation
Reading their poems to Vassar girls,
Being interviewed by *Mademoiselle*,
Having their publicity handled by professionals.
When can I go into an editorial office
And have my stuff published because I'm weird?
I could go on writing like this forever . . .

I finished quickly, ripped the sheet out of the typewriter, put it in an envelope, addressed it to a magazine, and—there was a knock on the door. It was Ginsberg. This gave me a nasty turn. The timing was weird, and in fact at other times I have run into Allen at the strangest moments.

He didn't say much. He stared owlishly, asked a few questions about how I was living, listened to my answers without making any comment, signed his book, and left. The signature was a skull and cross-bones with a halo over the skull, and the name Allen Ginsberg above an address in Paterson, New Jersey—William Carlos Williams country.

*

My own immediate task was to fulfill the course requirements for the Ph.D. At the same time I was teaching two or three nights a week, downtown at the New School and uptown at Columbia. At the New School I was lecturing on modern poets; at Columbia I was teaching composition. In both places my students were much the same—younger people who were trying to finish a degree at odd hours while holding down a job, and "continuing education" people who had returned to school after a life of business or raising children. They were grateful for anything they might receive, and this was fortunate, for I was a poor teacher. Five years of editing books had taught me nothing; I had done no research and had no information to impart; as my knowledge of literature was superficial, I was not able to make connections and concentrate on what was important. So in class I fell back upon paraphrasing the texts.

I was learning to teach at the expense of the students, but maybe there is no other way. On the elementary school level, "teaching method" courses may produce capable teachers, but there is no method for teaching well in universities. There is only an accumulation of knowledge through hours spent in the library, and learning to talk about what you have read. You are carrying on your own education in public, while the students fidget, yawn, and sleep.

XXXIII

I was writing poems and asking myself why.

As America emerged from the post-war apathy, the Eisenhower era, moving into a political atmosphere that would be violent and experimental, the poets, too, were beginning to rebel against conventional forms and the impersonality of the previous decade. At first in isolation, then two or three together, then in groups, the poets were breaking with academic rules and making their own, or having no rules at all.

After years in which there had been no questioning of principles, the poets—not the critics—began to raise radical questions. I too was beginning to examine my ideas. Why was I trying to write poems? What did I think poetry was? This is what I thought at the time—

*

If you examine what you really think, you will find yourself in a lonely place. But if you are serious about it—and if you're not, you aren't a poet at all—you must get to that place sooner or later. The sooner the better.

In America, success is the worst temptation for the writer, as it is for other men. At several points in my life I have seen rising clearly before me an opportunity to *belong*. I have met some of the more important literary men of my time, and they gave me to understand that they would be glad to help me in some way. But a voice within me, like Socrates' sign, said "Flee for your life!"

I know too much about literary life. I know by what means, by what steady cultivation of his betters, by what obsequiousness in print and out of it, the mediocre writer gets himself a name. As Huxley said, fame, the last infirmity of noble mind, is the first infirmity of the ignoble. The need of fame has turned many a decent man into an envious, spiteful, vanity-ridden, self-deluding wretch. And what does he have to show for it? A handful of reviews.

The poet's task is to tell the truth. And, of course, he must have talent. His only real satisfaction is in the writing of poems—a dull-seeming procedure in which he sits down facing a blank wall, and smokes, and from time to time scratches on a sheet of paper. There have been plays about piano-players and painters, but the writing of poetry is least suitable for dramatic representation.

It is getting harder and harder to write a poem. That is, I can start one well enough—but how to finish?

I used to be able to begin and finish a poem. I found that the poem was directed by certain external forces toward a certain end. But one day I found that ideas were better expressed in prose. No, it was more than that. I found that I no longer wished to please.

The reader has certain stock responses to ideas, and certain responses—not very strong, perhaps, but operative nevertheless—to metaphor, meter, and rhyme. A poem that satisfies his stock responses is "good"; a poem that does not is "bad". I find myself wanting to write bad poems—poems that do not depend on stock responses. I want to write poems that will not please. Recently I have been learning to write this new kind of poem. The most important change is in the content (whether one writes "in form" or "out of form" is not an essential question—it is a matter for simpletons to worry about, and of course it is the only question that reviewers feel competent to discuss).

Instead of statements which reassure the reader by their familiarity, or shock him by their strangeness—instead of opinions, there are only images and reverberations.

I can never finish these poems. I wrestle with them and leave off when I am exhausted. Frequently, all that remains is a handful of phrases.

The difficulty is that, to write this new kind of poem, which springs mainly from the subconscious, I must work not at technique, but at improving my character.

How much easier it is to settle on a certain style, to write a certain poem over and over again, publishing books of the same poems every four years!

There is this to be said for not being a professional man of letters—you can do as you like. What have you got to lose?

Work is all well and good, but what you pray for is inspiration. That is, one day when you sit down and wrestle with a poem, you find that you are wrestling with an angel. Then all the phrases flow together; the unfinished poems lying in the back of the closet rush and fly together. They are changed into something that you have not logically conceived. At such moments, which are rare enough, you are not writing but assisting at the birth of truth in beauty.

Of course, to some people this is all nonsense. To a deaf man, music does not exist; to a blind man, there are no constellations in the sky.

No, poetry is not dying, and verse is not a dying technique. Those who have said that it is, perhaps wishing that it might be, were writers of prose, and some of them were critics. They have congratulated themselves prematurely. A great deal of criticism is nothing to brag about, if the criticism has been an end in itself. And criticism in the last forty years has been largely an end in itself, a bastard kind of art, a kind of theatricals for shy literary men. I have known critics who were actors at heart, giving their own impersonations of Raskolnikov, or Donne or Freud. Next week, *East Lynne*.

What is most disappointing about criticism is that when you examine the critic's method, under the appearance of sweet reasonableness there are only prejudices and taboos. The critic's art depends on an exertion of his personality, an unstable quality. Now, poets and novelists and playwrights also use their personality, but from this they extract certain definite objects—the poem, the novel, the play. They deal in facts. But the critic deals in opinions.

An age of prose? All that prose has been a sympton of culture, and the culture was not directed to any serious purpose.

New Lines for Cuscuscaraway
and Mirza Murad Ali Beg

". . . the particular verse we are going to get will be
cheerful, dry and sophisticated".

T. E. Hulme

O amiable prospect!
O kingdom of heaven on earth!
I saw Mr. Eliot leaning over a fence
Like a cheerful embalmer,
And two little Indians with black umbrellas
Seeking admission.
And I was rapt in a song
Of sophistication.
O City of God!
Let us be thoroughly dry.
Let us sing a new song unto the Lord,
A song of exclusion.
For it is not so much a matter of being chosen
As of not being excluded.
I will sing unto the Lord
In a voice that is cheerfully dry.

★

When you are dealing with poetry itself, all these other
matters—the question of an audience, fashions in criticism,
the envy and malice that lie in your way like stumbling-
blocks—these all vanish. And the question of how to write
also vanishes.

(This last is uneasy. The question of how to write only
seems to vanish—it is still there; the writer is always
concerned with technique, though in the act of writing he
may not think consciously about it.)

When we have understood the social and psychological conditions that affect an artist's life and form his ideas, we still have not understood the impulse and nature of art itself. After all, many people have unusual lives, but very few are artists. Why does a man choose to be a writer? And why poetry?

He doesn't choose—he is moved by the rhythms of speech. Certain people have a physical, visceral way of feeling that expresses itself in rhythm. Some people play music, others dance, and others—who are attracted to words—utter lines of verse. These are the poets.

The rhythms of poetry rise from the unconscious. This is not generally understood, even by critics who write about poetry. Before a poet writes a poem, he hears it. He knows how the lines will move before he knows what the words are.

Descriptions of poetry by men who are not poets are usually ridiculous, for they describe rational thought-processes. For example, in the novel *Keep the Aspidistra Flying*, George Orwell describes a poet at work—putting one idea logically after another, choosing the next word, image, and rhyme. This is completely false; prose may be written in this way, but not poetry. A poet begins by losing control; he does not choose his thoughts, they seem to be choosing him. Rhythms rise to the surface; a fraction of a moment later the necessary words fall into place.

Poets agree that rhythm is of the first importance. Paul Valéry, for example, describes the physical state of a man on the threshold of poetry:

> I had left my house to find, in walking and looking about me, relaxation from some tedious work. As I went along my street, which mounts steeply, I was *gripped* by a rhythm which took possession of me and soon gave me the impression of some force outside myself. Another

rhythm overtook and combined with the first, and certain *strange transverse* relations were set up between them.

This was more strange, Valéry says, than anything he could have expected of his "rhythmic faculties"—meaning his will, his rational mind. The rhythms rising from the unconscious seem to arrive from outside. In former ages poets were often "visited" in this manner, and their utterances were regarded as divine truths. But the world has grown rational, and no head of state would consult a poet—except as a prop under the spotlights on a public occasion. Instead, it is the physicists who hand down our oracles.

★

When we try to explain poetry and defend it, we forget that it needs no defence, for poetry is a form of reality with certain definite powers. There is no substitute for the form and sound of a true poem. The poem is unique, therefore it exists. And the more powerfully it exists the less possible it is to explain it—that is, to replace it with prose.

Poetry is essentially mysterious. No one has ever been able to define it. Therefore we always find ourselves coming back to the poet. As Stevens said, "Poetry is a process of the personality of the poet." This personality is never finished. While he is writing the poet has in mind another self, more intelligent than he. The poet is reaching out to the person that he would be, and this is the poet's style—a sense of reaching, that can never be satisfied.

XXXIV

I had to write a dissertation for the Ph.D. I wanted to write on Heinrich Heine, but my adviser asked if I knew German, and when I said that I knew very little he told me to find another subject. If he had told me to go away and learn German I would have done so. But in the 'fifties advisers wanted to get the job done with as little trouble as possible, and students did not insist on having their own way.

Then I hit upon James Hogg, the Ettrick Shepherd. Hogg was a Scotsman who, at the beginning of the nineteenth century, wrote poems, stories and novels. He was a self-taught peasant and like Robert Burns had first-hand knowledge of folklore and a lively belief in the supernatural. Unlike Walter Scott, who adopted rationalistic ideas, invented the stage Scotchman, and spread romantic pictures of Scotland throughout the world, Hogg remained true to his peasant origins. He had written one novel that was a masterpiece. *The Private Memoirs and Confessions of a Justified Sinner* was not usually listed in courses of English literature, for it escaped the Establishment net, but it was one of the great novels in the language.

In the *Justified Sinner* Hogg created a very Scottish Devil—Gil Martin, a close friend with a taste for theological disputation. The character of the hero is even better—a man who thinks he has been elected, or "justified", and that therefore he is free to carry out every wickedness without fear of punishment. James Hogg's revealing of the mind of a fanatic has never been surpassed, and at the present day, if we substitute our political for his religious terms, the *Justified Sinner* is still an astonishing parable.

I had scarcely settled on this subject when I had a stroke of luck—I was awarded a prize that sent me to Italy for a year. (In America, prizes are awarded to artists on condition that they leave the country.) Free of the need to teach for a living, I would have the time to write my thesis. I would also be able to travel to Scotland and do some research in James Hogg's life and works right on the spot.

In Italy, surrounded by the monuments of Catholicism, I read in the literature of Scottish Calvinism. Also, I studied the hidden, unchristian side of Scottish life. In the course of pursuing James Hogg I gained some curious information about ghosts, witches, and fairies.

★

One night in Scotland, in the company of a friend and his wife, and a young girl who was travelling to meet her boyfriend, I drove into the West Highlands, passing by Stirling Castle and through Glencoe, arriving at last on the coast near Oban, where, to my astonishment, there were gardens of flowers and the sun was shining. This was in the afternoon; at twilight we came to the house where we were to stay for the night. My friends had an invitation from a Scottish minister, and he turned out to be a dour man. His house was only an appendage to the old estate; we were not to stay there, he said, but at the old manor, a much larger house that had been used by the ministers a hundred years ago when the kirk was more presumptuous. Saying hardly a word, he led the way to this big house, unlocked the front door, and showed us into a room where we were to sleep. There wasn't a stick of furniture in it, only bare boards and a fireplace. Then he left. My friends left soon after with the young woman who was going to meet her friend about twenty miles away, and as night fell I was standing in a big empty room, in the West Highlands, in a manor house where no one had lived for many years.

The house began to creak and I imagined there was some-one upstairs in one of the rooms listening and waiting. No sooner conceived than the fancy began to clothe itself and to move, coming to the head of the stairs. It was in the form of a woman—everyone to his ghost, but if I were to meet one it would be a woman's. Therefore I decided to go out of the house, for it would be better surely not to meet the thing inside a walled place. But when I was outside I was no longer sure, for the darkness was thick, with shadows of trees and a hill looming up. I felt that a ghost outside would be just as unpleasant, and I have never been able to decide whether it would be preferable to meet the dead inside a house or outside it—for in the house you could at least hope to get out, but if you were to meet a horrible thing in an open place, where else could you hope to go?

I decided to postpone the answer by keeping my body in motion and climbing the hill in the dark, which was a foolish thing to do, for I could not see my footholds. Never-theless, I arrived at the topmost ridge without breaking my neck and there, instead of being cheered up, I came upon a statue as large as a man, with a tin hat and a rifle, butt up, that he was leaning on, and a dedication to a dead regiment of soldiers who had been killed in the Great War. I went down the hill again, on the other side, and came into what must have been, I think, one of the oldest graveyards in Scotland. The moon had come out from behind the clouds and I could see all the tilted headstones and sunken hollows. There was no comfort here for the faint of heart. Then, looking to the left, I saw a flat green meadow shining in the moonlight and, beyond it, a straight white road. The road was civilized, and if I walked along it I would not run into any spectres. I was starting toward it across the flat meadow when into my head flashed something I had read about when I was doing the research for my thesis. In Scotland these flat green meadows by moonlight were bogs, and many a wanderer had been misled and had tried to cross such a place, and had sunk out of sight never to be found again. So I did not try to cross it, but made my way back to the house by another path, and in a while my friends returned and we unrolled our sleeping bags by the fireplace. This may be one of the only instances on record in which research for a Ph.D. thesis has saved a man's life.

★

When I came back to New York I turned in 400 pages to my Ph.D. committee. Two of the readers suggested revisions which I carried out. Then the dissertation went to Lionel Trilling, who wanted to reject it altogether. He advised me to find another subject. If I stayed around Columbia for a few years I might be able to find one.

It was a little late for this advice, for Trilling had been on the committee that approved my choice of James Hogg. I tried to find out what his objections were exactly, but all I could gather was that he did not think Hogg was important.

As Trilling did not explain his attitude, I have to speculate about it. James Hogg was a Scot. Trilling patterned himself on English models, and the English have never thought much of the Scots. Trilling had written a book on Matthew Arnold, and Arnold typically had remarked that the Scottish poet Burns was too nationalistic, by which he meant Scottish. I might have expected that Trilling would not like what I wrote about James Hogg, and that he would not understand the greatness of the *Justified Sinner*. In the Eng.-Lit. establishment certain authors are recognized as major; the rest are expected to stay in their place.

But something else seemed to be on Trilling's mind. He asked me to explain my method of teaching. I think what was really bothering him was that I wrote poems. Professors such as Trilling, who are essentially middle-class, feel uneasy with poets. They think that poets are unbalanced. They don't mind this if the poet is dead—to the contrary, the job of the professor is to explain the dead poet, how peculiar he was. But they don't know what to make of a living poet in front of them.

If the poet writes a dissertation full of unbalanced impressions, then they can deal with it. They will tell him that he is unsuited for a life of scholarship. But suppose the poet produces a conventional piece of research with footnotes?

Trilling had no grounds for rejecting the work I had done. It was acceptable by Ph.D. standards. But he distrusted poets, so he rejected it anyway.

This was too high-handed for even Columbia to stomach, and the head of the committee spoke to Trilling, and he withdrew his objections.

I went on with the defence of the dissertation. Two days before the defence, for my own amusement I read a book that described the Tay Bridge catastrophe. A hundred years ago in Scotland the Tay Bridge fell down in a gale, taking a train with it. A ridiculous poet named McGonagall wrote a poem on the subject. The first question at my defence came from Gilbert Highet, who said, "Some of the bad lines by Hogg that you quote reminded me of McGonagall." I said, "Yes, the poet of the Tay Bridge catastrophe." After this I had no trouble, for the other examiners, who could hardly have heard of McGonagall, must have thought I knew everything there was to be known about Scotland.

The dissertation was later published as a book in Edinburgh and New York.

Columbia College, so near to the market-place, was no place for a poet, and the distrust of poetry that was so evidently a part of Trilling's mind was passed on to his favourite students. They became businessmen of literature—critics, reviewers, publishers of books. They flourished in

New York and are still flourishing at the present time. If ever they think of poetry at all, it is with the contempt they learned at Columbia.

★

I was a writer with a Ph.D. At that time they were not as common as they are now, and if a writer had a job in a university he was expected to teach "creative writing" and to defer to scholars and critics. Now, of course, every English department has its poets and novelists.

First were the scholars—men, as Randall Jarrell said, who used to prove that "the Wife of Bath was really an aunt of Chaucer's named Alyse Perse". Then came the critics, and the scholars tried to keep them out. Some of the critics wrote stories and poems, but in order to establish their respectability they gave this up and put their energy into explication. Then came the writers, and the critics tried to keep them out: "Go away, pig! What do you know about bacon?"

Writers now have a place in the system. I wonder if we, in our turn, will try to keep anyone out?

Working in a university is a living. But I would have this written above the gate: "If you don't want to teach, stay out!" Universities are not for people who regard teaching as a burden and begrudge every hour given to it. A man who is paid to teach had better like teaching, for it is deadly work otherwise, and besides he will be doing harm to the students.

I don't mean that a man should neglect his writing in order to teach—to the contrary, this is what he must not do, for it is his writing that makes him an exceptional teacher. But, on the other hand, if he is resentful because he has to teach, then he has no place in a university. There

205

are writers and artists who need to live in secrecy, whose ideas might be spoiled by exposure, for whom analytic thinking could be truly harmful. These people had better not teach. I cannot imagine what Whitman, for example, would have done in a university.

For a writer who is able to teach, the university offers freedom to write as he likes—no small thing. Consider novelists who make a living by writing articles for magazines, and poets who have to go everywhere in costume. These people have very little real freedom.

The danger for the writer in the university is that he may become an "educator". He may get so much satisfaction from lecturing, conferring with students, becoming involved with their personal "problems", working on committees and being concerned about the fate of the university, that at the end of the day he will feel that he has done a day's work. A sense of social virtue can be more dangerous to a writer than private vice. Vice may drive a man to create something, if only to compensate for his guilt, but an artist who feels that he has justified himself by some other activity —good works of one kind or another—will no longer produce works of art. As Yeats says:

> . . . I had surrendered myself to the chief temptation of the artist, creation without toil. Metrical composition is always very difficult to me, nothing is done upon the first day, not one rhyme is in its place; and when at last the rhymes begin to come, the first rough draft of a six line stanza takes the whole day . . . I had found the happiness that Shelley found when he tied a pamphlet to a fire balloon.

So writers begin to pride themselves on their concern for their students and their service to the university, and no longer write. The university makes it easy for weak artists

206

to stop producing altogether. If it is said that this is no great loss, I can hardly disagree.

From the point of view of the university, artists are very desirable. They have a body of knowledge that no one else has: a first-hand knowledge of process, the way a thing is made. This is what they should be called on to impart to their students. They should not be called on to teach "painting" or "creative writing" as they so often are, for this is likely to exhaust their own creativity. They should teach the same subjects as everyone else—but the manner of teaching will be different. They shouldn't be in charge of workshops where students are trying to write or paint— they should be discussing ideas, telling their students about unusual books, arguing with them—in short, turning them into intellectuals.

The difference between the writer and the scholar as teacher will be in the writer's knowledge of process, his ability to make the student understand a work from the inside out—as an organism rather than an object. Writers can explain the structure and style of a work better than scholars, who for the most part have no interest in these matters. A writer can throw himself into a poem, novel or play as though he himself were creating it, and involve the student in the process of re-imagining the work. No true work is ever finished, and the man who explains a work as though it were still going on has the best understanding of it.

The man who himself composes or paints must be involved with the ideas of other men—even ideas in the distant past. He uses ideas, and exemplifies them by his work, and makes them new. Such men are among the best teachers.

XXXV

Robert Bly grew up on a farm in Minnesota and went to St. Olaf's College—the only other person I knew of who had gone to St. Olaf's was the Great Gatsby—then to Harvard, and had spent a few years thinking for himself. When I met him in New York his outer garment—the blue or grey business suit that even poets were wearing in the 'fifties—disguised a seething mind. He bought a Viking helmet with horns and contemplated wearing it to poetry-readings.

Bly was dissatisfied with nearly everything that had been taking place recently in American poetry and was looking for new ideas. He had been reading modern Spanish poets in particular. His own writing up to this point was typical of the 1940–1950 younger poets; he had been as able as anyone to write rhymed stanzas in literary language, but now he was growing irritated with this and searching for new ways of poetry in the writings of

Pablo Neruda . . . Garcia Lorca and Cesar Vallejo; in the Swedish tradition, Ekelof, in the French Char and Michaux, in the German Trakl and Benn—all of them writing in what we have called, for want of a better word, the new imagination, and making contributions to that imagination as enormous as Eliot's or Pound's and with a totally different impact, and on totally different roads.

Bly wanted poems that would not explain everything in the plodding, rationalistic way of the poetry of the 'forties. The new poems would be based not on English tradition, nor upon the—in Bly's opinion—exclusive, snobbish, psychically crippling ideas of critics such as T. S. Eliot and Allen Tate. Away with abstract language! Down with literary writing! Bly wanted writing in images, and the images must be new.

His description of the new images, however, was vague. He thought that the Imagists had been merely making pictures, and the images of the French surrealists came out of trivial associations, they lacked depth. The new image would be "deep". Bly found the Spanish surrealists more to his taste.

An imagination, a content, a style exists that has a magnificence of suggestion and association. I think it is mistaken to think that if we work in this style our works will resemble Eliot's or Pound's. Two things make me think different. First, some profundity of association has entered the mind since then. Freud's ocean has deepened, and Jung's work on images has been done. To Pound an image meant "Petals on a wet black bough". To us an image is "death on the deep roads of the guitar" or "the grave of snow" or "the cradle-clothes of the sea."

What would be the difference between Bly's use of surrealistic images and the old kinds? It was easy to see what he was against, but not so easy to see what he would make that would be new. That would depend on the quality of the life of the poet himself. If this surrealism were new, it would be so because it was written by men who were not French or Spanish, but American. So, at the same time that Bly's new magazine *The Fifties* spoke of neglected *avant-garde* traditions in Europe, South America and China, it was furiously American, printing poems that spoke of American earth, farm landscapes and highways. It was a curious, and at times awkward, combination of eclectic theorizing and local colour.

In his own poems Bly seemed to be trying to reconcile
the irreconcilable.

> the gold animals, the lions, and the zebras, and the
>   pheasants,
> Are waiting at the head of the stairs with robbers' eyes.

He asked for a poetry that would include "the dark figures
of politics, the world of street cars, and the ocean world"—
by the ocean he meant "this profound life", a life of the
spirit. It is easier to call for spiritual life than to represent
it in poems, and yet he was beginning, in certain poems
about Minnesota, to give the sensation of his ideas.

> How strange to think of giving up all ambition!
> Suddenly I see with such clear eyes
> The white flake of snow
> That has just fallen in the horse's mane!

My tastes in poetry were frequently different from Bly's.
I thought that some of the South American poems—maybe
as a result of translation into English—were just a series of
ecstatic exclamations. The poem was in a rapture with itself;
it would finish abruptly and seem to be be waiting for the
reader to say, "Astonishing! Fantastic!" The reader was
expected to be continually in a posture of amazement.

> The eye of a pistol wept dark tears,
> And smiles came from the onion.

Maybe there was some resonance to the images, but I
thought you would have to be in Chile to feel it. You
couldn't just transplant objects or turns of speech from one
culture to another—they didn't take. South American
surrealists might be deep, but translated into English they
were not interesting.

Also, poetry is an experience rather than a statement—

prose is for statements—and some of the poets Bly recommended seemed to be merely talking.

> Grief, my great laborer,
> Grief, be seated,
> Be still,
> Let us be still a little you and I,
> Be still,
> You are finding me, you are proving me . . .

But the ideas brought forward in *The Fifties* were
stimulating—at least they were more useful to poets than
what you could find in *The Hudson Review* or *The New
Yorker.* Though I would never write in the manner of the
Spaniards, Germans or Scandinavians Bly was publishing,
my writing was sharpened by our talks. Besides, the icono-
clasm was refreshing; we agreed vehemently about things
we did not like.

While praising the poets he admired, some of whom were
obscure, Bly attacked the poets he disliked, especially those
who were entrenched, and so he made enemies. Also, as
an editor he seemed unable to play the game according to
the rules agreed upon by editors of literary magazines. It is
practically unheard of for one editor to criticize another's
magazine, for all have to make a living. This is particularly
true in New York. Not only do they agree not to criticize
one another for practical reasons, but also they are linked
by friendship and even by marriage. If an editor has a wife
with literary ambitions, her name will soon appear on the
masthead of another magazine as one of their editors. This
is the Liberal Establishment, and it resembles the foreign
policy of the United States—as they are Liberal, whatever
they think must be right. These Liberals pride themselves
on having independent opinions about Civil Rights, foreign
movies, the war in Vietnam, hard-edge painting, *et cetera*—
but they all have the same ideas. The article that appears in

Commentary could just as well have appeared in *The New York Review of Books*, and they do not print anything of which they would not all approve.

This, on the other hand, was Bly's style:

AWARD

The Order of the Blue Toad is herewith awarded to Norman Cousins, editor of the *Saturday Review*, for putting out a boring, stupid magazine. His list of reviewers is enough to make anyone die of boredom—Granville Hicks, Doris Betts, Ben Ray Redman, Alma Lutz, Vincent Sheean, Lynn Montross, Stanley M. Swinton, *et al.* Why waste paper on such junk? The only good things the *Saturday Review* has published in the last five years were Schweitzer's atom-test appeal, and Ciardi's blast against Anne Morrow Lindbergh. However, someone soon quenched Ciardi's ardor; and his department has now settled down to the same level of mediocrity as the rest of the magazine.

Such remarks were insulting, and Bly's habit of mentioning the social or political implications of a poem struck some people as being in very poor taste. Writing was a game played by gentlemen, and to bring in personalities or to argue about politics was as unwelcome as a serious discussion at a cocktail party.

Poets who published in *The Fifties* were soon thought of as a group, for people are not happy unless they can label everything. I do not think that the *Fifties* poets—later, of course, the *Sixties*—were cohesive enough to be called a group, but they did have qualities in common. They differed from poets such as Nemerov, products of the New Criticism, in that they wished to speak with a personal voice; and differed from the Beat and confessional poets in that they wished to write about something more than the surface of life. They wanted to discover "deep" images. Their poetry would represent the unconscious.

The poems of James Wright, Robert Bly, Donald Hall, John Haines, Galway Kinnell, William Stafford, David Ray, and others, were a continuation of the "modernist" experiments of Pound, the Imagists and the Surrealists. The *Fifties* poets imported models from Germany, Scandinavia, Spain and South America. There was even a Minnesotan way of writing a Chinese poem. As I describe it, this movement may not seem new, but actually it was, in the sense that it was continuing an experimental movement that was never fulfilled in America.

During the 'thirties and 'forties poetry in America and Britain turned its back on the modernism of 1910, the experimentalism of the young Pound, Stevens, Cummings and Williams. Due to the New Criticism, poetry in the United States became a formalistic imitation of metaphysical verse, or under the influence of Auden a retailing of journalistic ideas. Modernism in English stopped before it had barely started, and the age that in other countries saw such poets as Pablo Neruda develop to their full stature, in the United States produced poetry of a conventional kind. It would be interesting to account for this retraction of the spirit; I think it was caused by the Depression, in the imagination of poets as well as in economics, but I must leave this for someone else to explore. The poetry of *The Fifties* was a renewal of the aborted modernism of the generation of 1910. There is not a great difference between some of the poetry of James Wright and this translation by Pound, in *Cathay*, 1915:

> Ko-jin goes west from Ko-kaku-ro,
> The smoke-flowers are blurred over the river.
> His lone sail blots the far sky.
> And now I see only the river,
> The long Kiang, reaching heaven.

Here is the naming of objects, then the imaginative leap from object to heaven, or to the interior world of the psyche, that is characteristic of Wright. In one of his recent poems Wright says:

Close by a big river, I am alive in my own country,
I am home again.
Yes: I lived here, and here, and my name,
That I carved young, with a girl's, is healed over, now.
And lies sleeping beneath the inward sky
Of a tree's skin . . .

A movement from the outward, objective world, toward the inner world of the psyche—this is practically Imagism as Pound described it. In an Imagist poem, Pound said, "one is trying to record the precise instant when a thing outward and objective transforms itself, or darts into a thing inward and subjective".

The *Fifties* poets were rooted in American landscapes, somewhat to the bewilderment of New York reviewers who could not believe that anyone took nature seriously. It was evident from the rise of poets such as these that American poetry would not be confined, as English poetry had been, by the opinions of a single literary capital. Minnesota and Seattle were as good places for poetry as New York and in some ways more stimulating.

In speaking of the *Fifties* poets I seem to have fallen into the cliché I have criticized—thinking of poets as a group. Every true poet is *essentially* different from other poets. Yet poets are not autonomous; they need other people and other people's ideas. It is true that a poet usually finds out about poetry by himself and begins his work in solitude, thinking that no one else is doing the same sort of thing. But then he discovers that other poets have been moving along the same line, for all have been influenced by the ideas of their time. For a while these people agree; they write letters to one another and meet and discuss ideas; they may publish a magazine, issue manifestos, and make anthologies. Then the group splits apart, each one going his own way. But their criticism of one another has had far-reaching consequences. So it was with Pound. But for the thinking he did in conjunction with T. E. Hulme, Ford Madox Ford, and Eliot, Pound would not have developed into a major poet. So it was with the "Oxford poets" of the 'thirties: Auden, Spender, MacNeice, and C. Day Lewis. Their poems were remarkably similar. They referred to the gasworks, and spies, and History; they spoke of the same heroes—Homer Lane, Marx and Freud. And so it is today. I believe that Denise Levertov no longer considers herself a follower of Olson, Ginsberg wishes no longer to be called Beat, and James Dickey is now loth to be associated with Bly; but at crucial moments these poets shared certain ideas with other poets and the moments determined the kind of poetry they would go on to write.

KEEPING ABREAST, OR HOMAGE TO PABLO NERUDA PERHAPS

Yesterday I met Thomas.
He was wearing a cloak and smoking marihuana,
and in his hip pocket he carried a volume
of Pablo Neruda.
"What is this, Thomas?" I said.
"Are you going to a masquerade?"

"I have cast off my old ways," he answered,
"and I advise you to do the same.
It is all testicles nowadays and light,
and a series of ecstatic exclamations."
Whereupon he struck the guitar
which he produced from his briefcase,
and began to sing of various mountains

215

in Chile. The stars figured prominently
and there was talk of the full testicles of night.

"Thomas," I said, "is this the new poetry?"

"It is the new world," he replied.

This kind of answer always leaves me feeling foolish.

Alas, I am outmoded.
But that is always the way—you read Rilke
and think you're safe for a while,
and then comes along a Neruda.
What did I ever do to Pablo Neruda?
I cannot take to hanging out in cafés,
and my Spanish is bad.
I am incurably addicted to the old kinds of poems.

The carob trees are preparing a corrida,
and I am the bull.
Death death death death . . .
They are chanting for the death of the old poetry.
O why was I ever taught anything?
Star, bird, light, and the breasts of Peruvian virgins—
these are, it seems, what is wanted.
The curved blade hangs in the air—
my carcass is roped to the heels of the mules.
Tomás, Tomás—a nice boy from Amherst,
a nice Jewish boy . . . if you could become a surrealist,
maybe I could too.
                        Tell me I still have a hope!

5

XXXVI

A man at the University of California at Berkeley wrote offering me a job. I didn't think I had much of a future at Columbia so I accepted and flew to San Francisco.

Strolling up the typically Californian street with its motels and liquor stores, to the university with its big trees, I felt that things didn't hang together. And though I lived in California for eight years, they never did. There would be picturesque characters, ranging from conservative old people to young radicals, but there would always be an absurdity to it all.

There are so many people who are happy living in California that there is no need to express their point of view; my own dissatisfactions may be of some comfort to the people who have found California not to be the paradise that Californians say it is.

The scenery is wonderful, what's left of it—brown hills, gardens full of flowers, the white city on its hills across the Bay. And of course the bridges. Everyone living in Berkeley wanted a view of the bridges. As professors were promoted in the English Department they would sell their houses and buy other, more expensive houses, further up in the hills so that they could look at the bridges. It was pontomania. Everyone was very conscious of his house, the view from the picture window, the additions he had made to the house —pointing with his pipe to the patio, "That came out of my book on Spenser."

Like most Easterners I had thought of the West as wide open spaces with people just moseying along, not caring about possessions. I should have paid more attention to

Westerns—cattlemen shooting each other in a quarrel over water and grazing rights. There was a man in Berkeley whose neighbour, an old lady, sent him a bill because the leaves of one of his trees had fallen on to her lawn. When he did not pay the bill she took to throwing stones at him. I myself raised beagles, and sometimes they howled; I had one of these old ladies for a neighbour, and she took to howling back. The hills of Berkeley are full of eccentrics who have retired from the world and will defend any intrusion upon their property or their privacy. It is not surprising that the student rebellions began there.

If I had expected the university to be more open-minded because it was in the West, in this too I could not have been more mistaken. In general, the curriculum was more conservative than in Eastern universities. The English Department was strong in Medieval and Renaissance literature, and not much interested in what was happening in the twentieth century. They weren't hostile—the modern just wasn't their field. No, it was more than indifference; I think they were afraid that if they loosened the curriculum the whole university would break away and drift south to Los Angeles, where everything is possible.

At a meeting of the English Department someone suggested that fifty years be taken away from the Anglo-Saxon period and given to the Medieval. A professor protested: "But Anglo-Saxon is our heritage." From studying English literature this man had actually come to believe that he was related to Beowulf.

So there was the dignified institution among its trees, and, half a mile away in Oakland, or to the east in the valleys, the real California began—streets on which used-car lots, churches, real estate offices, funeral parlours and hardware stores jostled one another. Nowhere is the split between what is called culture and the way we actually live more apparent than in California. Thought was a separate world, and the young found it hard to reconcile the university with the desert in which they lived.

California is a country of extremes, conservative or radical, and the gradations of human thought and behaviour, the discriminations that make for truth, do not exist. There is a confusion of art and life, no one knows exactly what he is or what he thinks, there is no history and no tomorrow. The art that is best suited to express this way of life is acting. The professors act like professors, the writers look like writers in the movies, and they elect an actor to govern them. Even death in California seems to be taking place in a movie. I had students who got married and divorced; some used drugs; others became political activists and were arrested—but few seemed able to grasp the reality of what was happening to them. I myself could not believe in the reality of the very earth I walked on. And in fact it was always threatening to slide.

XXXVII

It is common for a man to make poems and stories out of his past, but writing may also show what he will do in the future. For years I had been writing poems about American landscapes and thinking about the West. It was inevitable that I should go there. As I had not been born in America, but had come to it from the outside, I had the enthusiasm of a convert. I believed in the legends that are drilled into American school children, which they later forget or think about cynically. To me the American landscape was still romantic. In American writing I liked best the works that had been written with a love for the very sight and touch of objects, works that wished to incorporate everything. *Huckleberry Finn, Leaves of Grass, The Great Gatsby*, the poems of Hart Crane—in these works the love of the author for the materials of American life, the sight and sound and touch of things, was apparent. In these writings America was the new Eden, and the beasts and flowers were still to be named.

And mossy scabs of the worm fence, heap'd stones, elder, mullein and poke-weed.

Among American poets Whitman had been most conscious of the landscape, and for years I had been brooding over his lines. He was the best and worst of poets, but it doesn't matter how badly a man writes; all that matters, as Hemingway said, is that he should get the good stuff out. "Song of Myself" was the greatest poem yet written by an American. I found Whitman's ideas often intolerable; celebrating progress and industry as ends in themselves was understandable in 1870, for at that time material expansion was also a spiritual experience, but in the twentieth century the message seemed out of date. The mountains had been crossed, the land had been gobbled up, and industry was turning out more goods than people could consume. Also, the democracy Whitman celebrated, the instinctive rightness of the common man, was very much in doubt. Now we were governed by the rich, and the masses were hopelessly committed to an economy based on war. It was a curious thing that a man could write great poetry and still be mistaken in his ideas.

Meditating my love of Whitman's poems and dislike of his prophecies, I had been thinking of writing a poem about him. Rather, he kept creeping into my poems. While I was still living in the East I had travelled with Robert Bly up the Hudson to Bear Mountain, and there we looked at the statue of Whitman by Jo Davidson. Within a few days I started a poem about it, but I didn't finish the poem until I had been living in California for some time. The fragments then cohered all at once—the way it happens with me if I'm lucky.

WALT WHITMAN AT BEAR MOUNTAIN

". . . life which does not give the preference to any other life, of any previous period, which therefore prefers its own existence . . ."
—Ortega y Gasset

Neither on horseback nor seated,
But like himself, squarely on two feet,
The poet of death and lilacs
Loafs by the footpath. Even the bronze looks alive
Where it is folded like cloth. And he seems friendly.

"Where is the Mississippi panorama
And the girl who played the piano?
Where are you, Walt?
The Open Road goes to the used-car lot.

"Where is the nation you promised?
These houses built of wood sustain
Colossal snows,
And the light above the street is sick to death.

"As for the people—see how they neglect you!
Only a poet pauses to read the inscription."

"I am here," he answered.
"It seems you have found me out.
Yet, did I not warn you that it was Myself
I advertised? Were my words not sufficiently plain?

"I gave no prescriptions,
And those who have taken my moods for prophecies
Mistake the matter."
Then, vastly amused—"Why do you reproach me?
I freely confess I am wholly disreputable.
Yet I am happy, because you have found me out."

A crocodile in wrinkled metal loafing . . .

Then all the realtors,
Pickpockets, salesmen, and the actors performing
Official scenarios,
Turned a deaf ear, for they had contracted
American dreams.

But the man who keeps a store on a lonely road,
And the housewife who knows she's dumb,
And the earth, are relieved.

All that grave weight of America
Cancelled! Like Greece and Rome.
The future in ruins!
The castles, the prisons, the cathedrals
Unbuilding, and roses
Blossoming from the stones that are not there . . .

The clouds are lifting from the high Sierras,
The Bay mists clearing.
And the angel in the gate, the flowering plum,
Dances like Italy, imagining red.

All the time I lived in California I felt that I was carrying
out a Whitmanesque experiment, trying to digest the
landscape he had written about—though he had travelled
no further west than the Mississippi. In spite of my antipathy
for the Californians, their mindless pleasure-seeking and
their fear and envy of anything that came from outside,
yet I felt that I could find words for the reality of the place.

This was only a feeling, and I could not talk to other people about what I felt.

I could not talk to the San Francisco poets. In the first place they were chauvinistic and wanted nothing to do with strangers. Moreover, they really believed in the definition of poetry as either academic or non-academic; by academic they meant connected with a university, and were suspicious of this. But the exclusion was not all on their side; I had no real wish to know them; I have never liked literary circles, cliques or clubs. I was happy to look at the San Francisco literary scene from across the bay in Berkeley.

There had recently been a "San Francisco Renaissance". It was here that Ginsberg wrote "Howl", and other poets were becoming known—Robert Duncan, Michael McClure, Philip Whalen, Brother Antoninus, Jack Spicer. Kenneth Rexroth had come to San Francisco years ago, and Lawrence Ferlinghetti ran the City Lights Bookshop and was publishing the poetry of Ginsberg, Gary Snyder, Denise Levertov, and other new poets. The poets of the "Renaissance" had come to San Francisco from elsewhere; they were now rebounding from San Francisco, to be published in the East and even in Europe.

Californian poets insisted vehemently that here, not the East, was where poetry was happening. To understand their chauvinism it is necessary to step back about twenty years. At that time there was a famous poet living in California— Robinson Jeffers—and younger poets were overshadowed by his fame. In the 'thirties anyone who thought about poetry in California thought of Jeffers. He was romantic and his poetry had all the appearance of passion. His poems walked on stilts; they were tragic and frequently bombastic. From his tower at Carmel, Jeffers brooded over the capes that protruded, like saurians, into the Pacific. He had no friends, apparently, but hawks and stallions. Though there were people in his long narrative poems they had no particular, human characteristics; they were modernized versions of an idea of Greek heroes and heroines. Jeffers spoke of fate and doom and predicted a time when civilization, which he detested, would vanish from the face of the earth and nature would sweep everything clean.

> Neither our present blood-feud with the brave dwarfs
> Nor any future world-quarrel of westering
> And eastering man, the bloody migrations, greed of
>   power, clash of faiths—
> Is a speck of dust on the great scale-pan.

At the time of the Second World War, Jeffers had said harsh things about America, showing his dislike of the war and distrust of democracy. Consequently his popularity had sunk, though it would have declined in any case, for people were tiring of the monotony of his passion.

The new poets of San Francisco were in reaction against Jeffers. He had made a reputation in the East—they would ignore the East; in fact, they would care nothing about reputations. Their poetry would be aimed at their friends, not at a literary audience. Where Jeffers had walked on stilts they would walk on naked footsoles. He had written in formal sentences, using grand words; they would make jokes. Jeffers' poems were intended for concert halls; their poems would be read in coffee shops. Jeffers' poems had been published on fine paper; their poems would be published on cheap paper, or not printed at all—just a crumpled sheet of writing pulled out of a pocket.

The poets of California—and, later, younger poets everywhere—had a new theory of poetry, though most of them were not aware that they had it. They were writing unstructured, "open", colloquial poetry which owed much to the open, rambling method of Pound's *Cantos*. In the *Cantos* there is no structure to speak of; Pound tells everything that comes into his mind as it occurs to him. Actual historical episodes, legends, myths, and anecdotes of the writer's own life, occur side by side—"Beer bottles on the statue's pediment!"—and the language accordingly ranges from literary to slang.

In the writings of the new poets, instead of feelings expressed in emotive language, there was an emphasis on particular facts. There was little attempt to move the reader directly; instead, he was given data from which he could extrapolate the experience the poet had in mind. These poems were really do-it-yourself kits. This, too, was due to the influence of Pound, who had filled the *Cantos* with particulars—excerpts from letters and documents, figures of armaments production, accounts of commercial and financial transactions, history in the words of the men who were making it. But, even more than to Pound, the emphasis on facts was due to the example of William Carlos Williams and the Objectivist poets of the 'thirties. These men had argued that poets should suppress their own subjective feelings and let nature speak for itself. By nature they meant not just trees and flowers, but garbage-cans as well. Poems were to be mirrors of actuality; any expression of personal opinion was only a distortion of the truth. Indeed, truth was external to the human mind. Though there might be ideas in a poem, the ideas should be only those the poet was compelled to have by the very nature of things. In Williams' famous phrase: "No ideas but in things."

> Plaster saints, glass jewels
> and those apt paper flowers, bafflingly
> complex—have here
> their forthright beauty, beside:
>
> Things, things unmentionable,
> the sink with the waste farina in it and
> lumps of rancid meat, milk-bottle-tops: have
> here a tranquility and loveliness . . .

This was the kind of poetry that was now being admired. In California especially poets were imitating Pound's *Cantos* and Williams' *Paterson*, and even the shortest poem recited in a coffee shop reflected some of the theory. It was colloquial and unfinished; it talked about the writer's life in its factual details, but without an expression of personality. In passing there might be a swipe at the System, a little sociology in the manner of Pound, a dash of anthropology.

One of the San Francisco poets sounded much like another —indeed, it was part of their theory not to have a style. The following lines were written by Michael McClure.

> The beautiful things are not of ourselves
> but I watch them. Among them.

> And the Indian thing. It is true!
> Here in my Apartment I think tribal thoughts.)

> STOMACHE!!!
> There is no time. I am visited by a man
> who is the god of foxes
> there is dirt under the nails of his paw
> fresh from his den.
> We smile at one another in recognition.
>
> I am free from Time. I accept it without triumph
>
> —a fact.

This passage might just as well have been written by Philip Whalen. The following lines are by Whalen.

> Tuned in on my own frequency
> I watch myself looking
> Lying abed late in the morning
> With music, thinking of Y.
> Salal manzanita ferns grasses & grey sky block
>   the window
>
> Mossy ground

228

I think what is thinking
What is that use or motion of the mind that
                             compares with
A wink, the motion of the belly

This poetry has been called confessional, but though the writers talked about their own experiences, their poems remained curiously impersonal. They did not really confess anything. Ginsberg was a truly confessional poet, but most of the younger poets, especially those who wrote in the manner of Williams, seemed to be revealing facts about themselves rather than their own individual, personal character. All their confessions sounded alike.

I did not think that I would get anything from the ideas of the San Francisco poets. Their writing was a way of life, a social activity—they were always talking to each other in their poems. Now, this might be a satisfactory way, but it was not mine. For better or worse, my writing has been a dialogue with another self whom I may never know, and this is essentially private, like a love affair.

In their poems I did not think that the words were important; they lacked passion. Their words were like the sound-track of a movie, an accompaniment to pictures of life rather than the thing itself.

Another characteristic of the San Francisco poets . . . as they faced the Pacific, they thought about China and Japan. Moreover, the mountains at their back seemed to divide them spiritually from the rest of America. They longed for the peace of the Orient; they wrote imitations of haiku and their poems echoed Zen Buddhism. Gary Snyder had lived in Japan and, it was said, he had studied under Zen masters.

Zen was "that state of mind in which we are not separated from other things, are indeed identical with them, and yet retain our own individuality and personal peculiarities". I couldn't understand this. How could you be identical with

229

anything other than yourself; and if you could merge in this way, how could you still be yourself? The writer spoke of the "intangibility, indefinability, non-thing-ness, non-abstractness, non-morality and non-rationality of Zen".

In poems this seemed to come down to describing the simple facts of physical existence or making jokes, especially nonsequiturs. There are probably as many varieties of behaviour in Asia as there are in Europe and America, but the Californian version of Asian philosophy seemed rather simple—it was an avoidance of thought. There was none of the concentration that is necessary in Buddhism, for example.

In search of light I went to one of the Californian philosophers recommended by the young. He began by saying that he had found the Truth. Up to this time it had been kept from the people by a conspiracy of the elders, but he would now reveal it. Every man felt that he was alienated, cut off from others and from the Ground of Being. But here was the Truth: God (*Atman*) was in every man himself, and this self could in no way be separated from God. What appeared to be Evil was only *Maya*, illusion, one of the masks of God. For God was always playing games, hiding himself and seeking himself behind the appearances of things. In time all would come round and God would reappear, and peace and love would reign. All that is necessary is to remember that God is in oneself, that therefore it is oneself that is God and has created everything, the sun and the moon and the stars, and oneself cannot be destroyed nor separated from oneself, and there is no need to care.

Was not God also in care? I asked. And in the feeling that oneself is apart from others?

Was not God also in the elders he spoke of, who kept back the truth? And if everything was going to work out anyway, what was the use of his philosophy?

No use, said the guru. It was a game. Everything we

230

thought or did was a game. Time, space, the whole universe, was a game.

And we left it at that.

XXXVIII

In Berkeley time went by like the seasons, with no marked changes. Sometimes the classes I taught were large lectures, a sea of faces, and sometimes they were a dozen students around a table. The department was large, with a few exceptional people—Bertram Bronson the eighteenth-century scholar, Ian Watt and Mark Schorer who wrote on the novel, Henry Nash Smith who had written a book on the Western hero. Among the younger faculty there was the English poet Thom Gunn, who rode a motor-cycle.

Gunn had studied under Yvor Winters at Stanford and, I thought, Winters had inhibited his talent. Winters was fiercely traditional; he had come to think that only regular, rhymed poems were acceptable, anything else was down-right dangerous. He saw immorality in Romantic poems and threats to life and limb in free verse. If the San Francisco poets were one extreme, Winters was another. I got a feeling that all over California there were people who had adopted or been driven to extreme positions.

For a while this thought did not bother me. I had books to write and teaching to keep me busy. But when the books were written and I began to look around, I saw that I was becoming isolated and that, if I didn't watch out, I might find myself living further and further up in the Berkeley hills—with a few narrow ideas like Winters, or an interest only in camping and fishing. As I have said, I did not have any affinity with the poets in San Francisco. I had one friend there who was a poet, George Hitchcock. He was publishing a magazine called *kayak*, but he seemed rather isolated; he had little to do with people such as Rexroth and Ferlinghetti; he managed to be autonomous.

Though writing was a private affair, I did not want an isolated life. So I started giving poetry-readings. I flew to Oregon, British Columbia, Minnesota, Michigan, Kentucky, Pennsylvania, Tennessee, New York. Most of the readings were arranged through the Academy of American Poets. You gave an hour's reading of your poems, and went to a party, and the next morning you were sent flying on your way or were driven to the next town. This was known as a poetry-reading circuit. If you were doing several readings one after the other, you began to hear your voice as an echo; it was hard to tell whether you were reading the poem at this moment or had read it yesterday. The audiences ranged from large to small, and you could never predict what the response would be. As a rule, the bigger the university the less happy the reading, for they were accustomed to having visitors and there was always someone to let you know it. Smaller places were more appreciative.

You meet some funny people on these poetry-reading tours. There is the man who has been told by the English Department that he is to take care of you. He doesn't know your work, and wouldn't like it if he did, but he's stuck with you. He deposits you at a motel and reappears at 6 o'clock accompanied by his wife and other members of the department. You all go to the best restaurant in town, for this will be paid for by the department. Your host asks if you'd like a drink. You say that you would, and everyone has a drink. Then, with a nervous look on his face, he asks

232

if you want another. He knows all about drunken poets—
Dylan Thomas once passed this way. If you say that you
don't, he's visibly relieved. Then the waiter takes the orders,
and everyone eats like a horse, especially the wife of your
host. The conversation staggers; they are under the impression that you want to talk about nothing but writers' lives—
what they have just published, who they are sleeping with,
how they have disgraced themselves.

At 7.45 you rise to go to the reading. At this point the
wife of your host says, "I'm terribly sorry but I can't be at
the reading. We couldn't get a baby sitter," and she waddles
off. She has eaten out more times this way, and has yet to
attend a poetry-reading.

*

BEFORE THE POETRY READING

Composition for Voices, Dutch Banjo, Sick Flute,
and a Hair Drum

I

This is the poetry reading.
This is the man who is going to give the poetry reading.
He is standing in a street in which the rain is falling
With his suitcase open on the roof of a car for some
reason,
And the rain falling into the suitcase,
While the people standing nearby say,
"If you had come on a Monday,
Or a Tuesday, or a Thursday,
If you had come on a Wednesday,
Or on any day but this,
You would have had an audience,
For we here at Quinippiac [Western, or Wretched State U.]
Have wonderful audiences for poetry readings."

233

By this time he has closed the suitcase
And put it on the back seat, which is empty,
But on the front seat sit Saul Bellow,
James Baldwin, and Uncle Rudy and Fanya.
They are upright, not turning their heads, their fedoras
    straight on,
For they know where they are going,
And you should know, so they do not deign to answer
When you say, "Where in Hell is this car going?"
Whereupon, with a leap, slamming the door shut,
Taking your suitcase with it, and your Only Available
    Manuscript,
And leaving you standing there,
The car leaps into the future,
Still raining, in which its tail-light disappears.
And a man who is still looking on
With his coat-collar turned up, says
"If you had come on a Friday,
A Saturday or a Sunday,
Or if you had come on a Wednesday
Or a Tuesday, there would have been an audience.
For we here at Madagascar
And the University of Lost Causes
Have wonderful audiences for poetry readings."

II

This is the man who is going to introduce you.
He says, "Could you tell me the names
Of the books you have written.
And is there anything you would like me to say?"

III

This is the lady who is giving a party for you
After the poetry reading.

234

She says, "I hope you don't mind, but
I have carefully avoided inviting
Any beautiful, attractive, farouche young women,
But the Vicar of Dunstable is coming,
Who is over here this year on an exchange program,
And the Calvinist Spiritual Chorus Society,
And all the members of the Poetry Writing Workshop."

IV

This is the man who has an announcement to make.
He says, "I have a few announcements.
First, before the poetry reading starts,
If you leave the building and walk rapidly
Ten miles in the opposite direction,
A concert of music and poetry is being given
By Wolfgang Amadeus Mozart and William Shakespeare.
Also, during the intermission
There is time for you to catch the rising
Of the Latter Day Saints at the Day of Judgment.
Directly after the reading,
If you turn left, past the Community Building,
And walk for seventeen miles,
There is tea and little pieces of eraser
Being served in the Gymnasium.
Last week we had a reading by Dante,
And the week before by Sophocles;
A week from tonight, Saint Francis of Assisi will appear
    in person—
But tonight I am happy to introduce
Mister Willoughby, who will make the introduction
Of our guest, Mr. Jones."

V

This has been the poetry reading.

In spite of all I have said against it, reading poems aloud may be useful. When you read to an audience you must come to terms with what you really feel. Reading a poem aloud is not an infallible test of its value; I have read poems that were liked by an audience, yet afterwards I had to discard them as worthless. But, in general, you can tell that the feeling in a poem is real if you can read it aloud with conviction. It is your own feeling of conviction that matters, rather than the response of the audience.

The reading that pleased me most was to an audience of "disadvantaged" young people in a vocational training school in Brooklyn. They were learning to be mechanics and were not accustomed to hearing poetry, so I read poems with a strong narrative or dramatic element. They understood everything perfectly. Their questions afterwards were about the relationship of poetry to life, how had I started writing poems, *et cetera*. I found them more intelligent about poetry than the middle-class boys and girls you find in colleges, with their lifeless expressions—the result of having always had more of everything than they wanted.

XXXIX

I had a year off from teaching. I travelled to Italy, but I wanted the sound of American, so I returned and spent the year in New York.

I had forgotten how difficult it is to live in New York, in a box up in the air. How do writers live in New York? What do they find to think about? A trip to the shoestore or delicatessen. Dogshit on the sidewalk. Then there are gatherings where, as Hemingway said, they try to derive nourishment from contact with one another like "angle-worms in a bottle".

But everything comes through New York; it is a vortex, and I suppose this is why people are willing to live there—to feel the excitement of life whirling round and passing through.

Donald Hall came in from Michigan. He had been assigned to interview T. S. Eliot, who was in New York for a while, practically incommunicado. Donald and Robert Bly and I were standing on a midtown corner, and the man who was with Donald was holding a tape-recorder. Bly suggested that he and I go along to the interview, though we weren't invited. But how to get in? We could say that we were technicians and handle the recording.

So we went to the apartment-house where Eliot was staying. The door was opened by the poet himself. "I see that you brought a posse," he said to Donald. He was hospitable. He made stiff glasses of whisky for the interviewer and the technicians. The new Mrs. Eliot was there also, a smiling, comfortable woman. I remembered what Eliot had said of marriage, that it was making the best of a bad job, and wondered what difference it would have made to his poetry and plays if he had met her earlier.

It is a pity that ideas depend so much on personal relationships. People come and go, and I like to think of ideas, poems, stories as permanent—but they aren't, for they depend on people. In fact, they are mostly about people, unless they are about God. In his later poems Eliot wrote about God.

He was sitting three feet in front of me, in profile,

237

answering Donald's questions. I was conscious that I was looking at the most important literary man of the last forty years. And one of the great poets in English. If the age were to be named after one man, it would probably be Eliot. This did not mean that he was the greatest writer of the age, for among real writers there is no competition—it is only second-rate minds that are always ranking poets as first, second, third, and so on. There is no way to prove that one good poem is better than another. In the republic of poetry all are equal. Yet some men have a historical importance that can be seen; they influence other people; they change the opinions of the age. Dryden had this importance; so had Dr. Johnson and Wordsworth. Since the 1920s Eliot had had it. That was not to say that he was the greatest poet of the age—who could say if Eliot or Yeats were the greater? Or Rilke? Or a dozen other poets whose names were not known beyond their own country. But Eliot had captured the *zeitgeist*, and it was sitting three feet in front of me.

It must have been apparent to Eliot that the "technical assistants" were nothing of the kind, for we had trouble with the tape-recorder, and laughed at his jokes, and after three whiskys one of the technicians fell off a chair. The noise is audible on the recording.

I left feeling that I had been exposed to a kind of radiation. In recent years there have been attempts to down-grade Eliot, mainly by disciples of Pound who think that if Eliot is a great poet then Pound cannot be, and in Pound's writings there are remarks that show that he was envious of Eliot's fame. The comparison does not do honour to Pound, nor can it lessen Eliot's greatness. For my part, I prefer Eliot. Pound has been a lyric poet, a disseminator of ideas, and a brilliant mimic of other men's styles. But his poems are not profound and, except in a few passages here and there, it is hard to discover a real identity. Most of

238

Pound's *Cantos* are like Blake's prophetic books; they are poetry if you subscribe to the theory that, as the author was a gifted poet, then everything he wrote was poetry. Otherwise, these works are a mess of ideas interspersed with lyric and narrative passages. Eliot, on the other hand, had the ability actually to create in images the things he was talking about, and architectonic power, the ability to draw things together. Eliot had an identity and it was recognizable in all he said—"In my beginning is my end". But I will leave such comparisons to those who have an interest in the rise and fall of reputations. As Bentley said, no man was ever written down but by himself.

★

Bly lived on a farm in Minnesota, and I went out there in the summer. The country was flat and hot, with fields of corn, oats, alfalfa, stretching away from the houses and barns. Now and then there would be a clump of trees, but the people who had come here from Norway hated trees and cut them down, so there was no shade between the deep black earth and the white sky. In the summer, heat gathered and lay on the earth like a blanket; then lightning flashed and it thundered. A livid, violet light flickered on the silos, and rain poured down in sheets. When it stopped you could hear water trickling from every surface and the sounds of small lives reviving along the furrows. The heat returned and the grasshoppers resumed their dry chirping, a note almost beyond the range of hearing, so continuous that you ceased to hear it, as though it were another voice of the earth itself, an extension of the rustling of green blades.

The farm was a quarter-section. Bly didn't work the farm; someone else did that. A poet's house was an oddity here in the middle of America; the people in Madison knew that a poet lived here and that strangers came from far away to visit. Whatever they thought about it, they didn't say. Farm people don't talk much, except about weather, crops, machinery. In a distant field you could see one or two men working from morning till night in silence. If you went into Madison there were few people on the streets. Then night came and solitary lights shone through the darkness.

Inside the house, in a room lined with books, we sat and talked. There were poems read aloud, and sometimes one of the men read something he had been writing and the others gave their opinions. James Wright read one of his new poems. He had begun, like so many others, with poems that were traditional. His early poems had been filled with echoes of E. A. Robinson.

> Soon we must leave her scene to night,
> To stars, or the indiscriminate
> Pale accidents of lantern light,
> A watchman walking by too late.
> Let us return her now, my friends,
> Her love, her body to the grave
> Fancy of dreams where love depends.
> She gave, and did not know she gave.

His new poems were different; you could have described the changes in American poetry in recent years just by listing the differences between Wright's first book and his new manuscript.

> In the Shreve High football stadium,
> I think of Polacks nursing long beers in Tiltonsville,
> And gray faces of Negroes in the blast furnace at Benwood,
> And the ruptured night watchman of Wheeling Steel,
> Dreaming of heroes.
>
> All the proud fathers are ashamed to go home.
> Their women cluck like starved pullets,
> Dying for love.

Therefore,
Their sons grow suicidally beautiful
At the beginning of October,
And gallop terribly against each other's bodies.

It started to lightning and thunder and the clouds burst. Then Wright decided to go to the outhouse, which was some distance away on the other side of a wire fence. He went out under an umbrella. Time passed and he still had not returned. We went out to look for him. He was standing on the other side of the fence, holding the open umbrella at his side, looking up at the raining sky. He was drenched to the skin. It seemed that he was not able to figure out a way to get back through the fence with the open umbrella, or a way to close it. So he just stood there. Maybe he liked being rained on, and was composing. There was an ecstatic look on his face.

One day we drove to a lake that we heard no one had fished for years, and we caught dozens of sunfish. The water was absolutely still and on the other side we could see the beginning of South Dakota. This was Indian country. At the end of the day's fishing I felt that I understood the Indians a little better. Hunting and fishing are enough; a man shouldn't have to do more than this; he shouldn't have to work. A man could be part of a natural cycle, killing and consuming what he killed, himself to be consumed in turn. It seemed perfectly right and natural.

At this time we were writing Indian poems. The Indian was being taken up again as a symbol. It was nostalgia, and something more: in their search for a way of life to identify with, poets were turning to an idea of the dark, suppressed American. We talked, I remember, about the "inner life". Some day someone will take the poems about Indians written by men as different as Bly and Snyder and discover what they were driving at. The Indian, I have no doubt, was as foolish as the white man, and the people who settled Kentucky would have wondered at our sympathy for howling savages. History and poetry are far apart; poems about Indians were a fantasy of sophisticated twentieth-century people who were trying to find ways out of the materialism that was everywhere around them.

XL

At Berkeley lines of students wound over the campus; they were registering for classes and being herded like sheep from one door to another. It seemed that life could go on like this forever at the university, detached from the world outside.

But it couldn't. Symptoms of disorder were appearing, nerve-tics. When the House Un-American Activities Committee came to San Francisco, students disrupted the proceedings until the police washed them off the street with a hose. Other students travelled to Mississippi and Arkansas, to take part in Civil Rights demonstrations and be put in jail; when they came back they were hardened reformers, and some of them were radicals, determined that the whole "System" must be brought down.

I observed one instance at first hand, though I didn't recognize it for the omen that it was. At Berkeley it was customary for all professors to teach the first-year composition course. This was an excellent idea, for it gave freshmen a chance to study with more experienced teachers as well as young instructors. In my class I had one student who was a problem from the start. He was unusually nervous. Early in the semester I assigned a reading from Gandhi in which he was explaining non-violent resistance, the reasons it had been necessary and the methods he had used. Shortly after this, the student vanished from the class. The next I knew, he was sitting under the campanile in the middle of the campus and refusing to leave. He was fasting in protest against military training. Then his father, who was an officer in the Air Force, came and took him away.

*

As early as May, 1964, Senator Wayne Morse warned against the war in Vietnam: "This illegal and unilateral course of action of the United States in South Vietnam could lead to a third World War." Others had spoken out; a handful of people were conscious that the United States had undertaken to interfere in a civil war in Asia and that the consequences could be disastrous.

The war struck me from the start as unnecessary, so when I was asked to sign my name to an ad that would appear in the *San Francisco Chronicle* protesting against U.S. participation in the war, I complied. There were sixty-three signatures, and the ad, calling for a conference to negotiate a settlement of the Vietnam War, appeared in the *Chronicle* on August 28th. Then a few of the people who had signed the ad were asked to come over to San Francisco for a press conference in order to explain their objections to the war. This was the new America, in which those who did not wish to support an undeclared war were called upon to justify their position.

Our meeting with the reporters was televised. Asked to give my reasons, I said that the war was immoral. This struck the reporters as irrelevant. One of them asked if I

243

didn't think that the President and his advisers knew more about what was happening in Asia that I did. I said that I knew only what I felt about the war, and was better able to know what I felt than any number of experts.

That evening the interview was on the six o'clock news. A few minutes later the phone rang. It was an anonymous call, long distance, and a man's voice said, "We're going to get you." I have always thought that all sorts of good things are going to come to me for something I have done, and my instinctive reaction was to ask, "Get me what?" But the voice's following remarks were explicit. I was to go back where I came from, I was no American, he had a son in Vietnam, etc. I said that if he had a son in Vietnam I would think he would want his son brought home. But no, it seemed the war couldn't be bloody enough to suit this parent. As he continued to make threats I told him that he was under a misapprehension—I was not a pacifist.

This exposure convinced me of the need to take more positive action, and in the following months I took part in several meetings protesting against the war. There is nothing that will encourage dissent as much as a feeble attempt to suppress it.

Was this treason? On the contrary. We were opposing the Johnson administration, which was subverting the Constitution. Johnson was using the Gulf of Tonkin resolution in order to escalate the war, without bringing it to a vote by the Congress. Putting aside his untrustworthiness—this was the man who had campaigned on a promise not to send Americans to Asia—the President had all the makings of a dictator. It would have been treason not to oppose him.

But though my conscience was clear on this point, opposing one's government is uneasy. General Grant once remarked, "The man who obstructs a war in which his nation is engaged, no matter whether right or wrong, occupies no enviable place in life or history." Grant was

244

writing about the war with Mexico. He was a young lieutenant when that war—much like the adventure in Vietnam—was begun. Grant thought the war with Mexico unjust—in his words, an example of a republic imitating the worst habits of European monarchies. Americans had provoked the war so that the President could present the Congress with a *fait accompli:* "Whereas, war exists . . ." The war was unjust, yet he went to it—following the guidons across the Rio Grande, hauling a cannon up to a church belfry. "The shots dropping among the enemy caused . . ." maggots and flies. So Grant made himself a name. In his old age, writing his *Memoirs* for the *American Century*, he apologized for his cowardice, pleading necessity.

As Milton says, necessity is the tyrant's excuse; it was President Johnson's. Also, it is the excuse of those who submit to tyranny—"The man who obstructs a war . . . occupies no enviable place." These words might have been offered as an excuse by the Nazis at Nuremberg. But the court decided that every man is responsible for his acts and cannot plead that he was just "following orders". We felt bound to oppose this war which had not been forced upon America but undertaken by the President and his advisers.

Nevertheless, I had a personal reason for feeling uneasy—I was a naturalized citizen; I had been given my citizenship in the army. A naturalized citizen never feels quite sure of his right to criticize the country that has "given him" his citizenship. If you are born in a place you belong there, whatever you do; but if you are naturalized you feel that you are under an obligation not to make trouble. This is wrong, of course, and if an American does not criticize the government he is failing in his duty toward it; nevertheless, I felt a certain guilt as I dissented.

Up to this time my opinions had been those of the majority. During World War II I felt like everyone else; I had no doubts about the necessity of that war. During the

245

McCarthy years I was tired and wanted to be left alone—in any case, I was not then called upon to feel, let alone do, anything. But now, as I had begun to be more personally involved in teaching and writing—as my style changed from traditional stanzas and rhymes to a free-flowing line that expressed my own ideas—I could not help being concerned, if only for the welfare of my poems. If I accepted the injustice of this war, how could I possibly speak on any subject? I think that many of the poets felt this way: it was mental freedom that was at stake, and in order to continue writing they would have to oppose the Johnson administration.

I was beginning to understand America. You have not understood America until you have been in a minority. It is then that you begin to realize how precarious freedom is; how it has depended, from the start, on a handful of people who spoke for what they considered to be right, against the weight of public opinion. The liberty that is taught in schools has been won at a great cost to individuals, not by the people at large. The majority are content to be ruled, and marched off to wars, and to stand by while atrocities are committed. What most people want is not to have to think for themselves.

At the end of one protest-reading a stranger rushed up as the speakers were leaving the platform. He was festooned with cameras; he'd been taking photographs under the delusion that there was something secretive about our proceedings and the F.B.I. didn't know who we were. He shouted, "What right do you have to criticize the government?"

Then he went on to cast aspersions on our virility. Such people are shocked to hear someone speaking out against injustice, while they themselves are silent. They feel accused; this arouses their sexual anxieties, and in order to get rid of them they project them on to the speaker. As this man mouthed his insults I wondered at him. Then I felt strangely touched, sorry for him, and grateful for the question, "What right do you have to criticize the government?" The question set a thousand voices ringing in my ears, and if I had any doubts about the rightness of what we were doing, they ceased from that moment.

★

The war and protest-readings were pushed aside by an event closer at hand—the Free Speech Movement at Berkeley, the first of a series of campus sit-ins, strikes and riots that have now become commonplace.

When the Fall term began, some of the students were picketing the *Oakland Tribune* in protest against what they said were discriminatory hiring practices. Then all student organizations received a letter from a dean of students stating that tables would no longer be permitted in the strip of university property at the Bancroft and Telegraph entrance and students would not be allowed to distribute literature, solicit funds, and advocate political action that would take place off the campus. The administration, represented by Chancellor Strong, stated: "The University will not allow students or others connected with it to use it to further their non-University political or social or religious causes, nor will it allow those outside the University to use it for non-University purposes." Clark Kerr, president of the university, said: "I don't think you have to have action to have intellectual opportunity. Their actions—collecting money and picketing—aren't high intellectual activity. . . . These actions are not necessary for the intellectual development of the students."

The students had a different idea. They did not think that a line could be drawn between "intellectual activity" and political action. On September 30th they set up tables in the Bancroft-Telegraph area and in front of Sather Gate.

247

They had been denied permits from the office of the Dean of Students, but they solicited funds anyway, in violation of university regulations. Administration representatives took the names of five students manning the tables and instructed them to report for disciplinary action. But more than five hundred students and protesters appeared. They filled the corridors of Sproul Hall, which was the administration building, and sat down, and two of their leaders, Mario Savio and Arthur Goldberg, stood on a narrow balcony shouting to passing students, urging them to join the sit-in. Savio presented a petition to the Dean of Students, signed by more than five hundred students, demanding that all five hundred "be treated exactly the same" as the five who were summoned, and that all charges should be dropped until the university "clarified its policy".

After some discussion between the administration and the students sitting-in, on the following morning at 2.40 a.m. the demonstrators left Sproul Hall. But that day a man named Jack Weinberg who was soliciting funds for CORE in front of Sproul Hall was arrested for trespassing. Weinberg went limp. The police brought in a car to remove him. About 180 students promptly lay down around the car and Mario Savio climbed on top of it, using the car as a platform from which to address the crowd. This situation continued for thirty-two hours, Weinberg remaining inside the car, being fed sandwiches and milk through a window.

The university was now dealing with an insurrection. The students packed the doors of Sproul Hall, and one of the policemen trying to prevent this was bitten on the leg. The Governor of California issued a statement in support of President Kerr and Chancellor Strong, calling for "law and order on our campuses". On October 3rd the Chairman of the Board of Regents issued a statement that "law and order" had been re-established on the Berkeley campus and that a faculty committee would review the situation and

248

make recommendations. He blamed the trouble on "a relatively small number of students, together with certain off-campus agitators".

After weeks of haggling the administration agreed that the students might use certain campus facilities for "lawful off-campus actions". But then Savio and Goldberg were told that they would have to answer charges for their part in the demonstrations. Thereupon, on December 2nd, Savio led a mass sit-in of Sproul Hall. He told the students, "You've got to put your bodies upon the gears and upon the wheels . . . to make it stop," and Joan Baez told them to go in with love in their hearts. They packed into the building.

At three the next morning the police started taking them out. They were given the choice of walking or being dragged. Most of them went limp and were dragged. From the basement they were loaded into buses and paddy wagons and taken off to jail. They were charged with failure to disperse, refusal to leave a government building, and resisting arrest.

There were more than eight hundred demonstrators arrested. This was, of course, the famous riot at Berkeley. Actually it wasn't a riot, but passive resistance. On the other side, Free Speech spokesmen charged "police brutality", claiming that the demonstrators were clubbed and kicked and had their arms twisted, hair pulled, etc.

Something new had come into American campus politics —direct political action. The public reaction to this was strong and, not just in Berkeley but across the country, it tended to be hostile to the FSM. Most people saw the students as a bunch of sheep being misled by professional agitators and Maoists. The public insisted on believing that only a small number of students were in sympathy with the Free Speech Movement, whereas in fact at times thousands of students had supported it, including members of conservative student organizations who felt that their own rights of free speech were being threatened along with the rights of the radical Left. There was a great deal of deliberate misrepresentation by the press and television services. I would see the classrooms empty and a huge rally taking place in Sproul Plaza, with speakers of all kinds, including respectable professors, but in the news broadcasts the cameras would dwell on the most dishevelled, hysterical speakers, and the news commentators would say that only a few students were involved and the university was functioning as usual. It is one thing to suspect that the news media are corrupt; it is astonishing actually to see lies being fabricated before your eyes.

Like many others, I had ignored what was going on until the final day when the students were taken to jail. I came over to the university as usual and saw a picket line with some of my students in it. One of them shouted, "Are you going to join us?" A few minutes later I saw the police carrying limp bodies out of Sproul Hall to the paddy wagons. Then I heard that bail had to be raised for these students, so impulsively I went up to my office. On the way I was passed by a group of students who were also heading for the English Department. Students? They were hairy and looked as though they hadn't washed in weeks. They filled the corridor of the English Department and conferred with the professors who had appeared in order to raise bail. The students were in command and authority had been turned upside down. I found myself making telephone calls to lawyers at the direction of a nineteen-year-old girl who seemed to know all about such business. I cannot explain our eagerness to hand over authority in this way, except that the spectacle of students being arrested and the campus in the hands of helmeted policemen put us instinctively on the side of the students. The police action brought thousands into sympathy with the Free Speech

Movement and put dozens of people to work composing pleas and gathering money.

That spring I found myself on a committee that had been formed to raise money for the bail bondsmen and meet the legal expenses of the arrested students. This was tedious work, and I envied the students, who at least were going through an interesting experience. At committee meetings I would have to sit still while one man explained legal business at length; another would speak of politics from the viewpoint of his experiences in Poland in 1910; another would reminisce about the 'thirties.

The students, on the other hand, had no obligations, and most of them had no plans. Some of them had read Marcuse, but more had seen *The Wizard of Oz*. They were not communists or anarchists—they were simply making up everything as they went along. They would throw themselves into a situation and see what developed and then ride along with it. Their politics were a happening, and they lived from one happening to the next. It was a way of life. Of course, they had certain consistent reactions against authority, but these could not be called a plan.

To hear an old-style Marxist analysing the student movement was therefore ridiculous. To sit dealing with figures and listening to professors explaining the movement, while there was no explanation—there were only voices in the Plaza, and the movement was what was happening—became for me a kind of torture. I don't know what the students who went to jail suffered, but I know that I suffered on the committee. The students were having all the fun, they were "doing their own thing", and I realized the trouble with older people was that we were not doing our own thing. (Of course, there were some intellectuals who put on an appearance of youth and seemed to think that everything "the kids" did was fine. They were relieved to hand over their intelligence to the young and abdicate responsibility, because they had never had any real part in their own generation.) I decided that political activity was no good—it would not persuade anyone—unless you yourself enjoyed what you were doing. The students were certainly enjoying themselves, but the rest of us were merely carrying out duties.

I decided it was time to do what I enjoyed. I might read poems aloud for political reasons, but I wouldn't deal with figures, not if the world were coming to an end.

When the Free Speech students had established their right to speak in the Plaza, a group started a crusade for the right to say "fuck". This was called the Filthy Speech Movement, and the public lumped both movements together. Anyone who wanted to discredit the Free Speech Movement could not have hit on a better way, begun by the students themselves. The Filthy Speech students said they wanted to use four-letter words because that was the way "poor people"— that is, black people—talked. A strange idea of black people! To these white middle-class children all black people were the same.

A more likely explanation is that these students had a fear of sex, handed down through generations of Puritan teaching. They wished to rid themselves of the fear, and believed that if they used the hidden words for sex, brought everything into the open and stripped men and women naked, they would remove the danger. If the relations of men and women could be thought of as only "fucking", then they need not be afraid any more. It is the hope of puritans that by speaking plainly they will remove the trouble of life.

Some people saw in the student rebellions a danger of total revolution. Intellectuals who had come from Europe feared a repetition of the German youth movements of the 'thirties which moved to the Right and found a *Führer*. The Germany-minded intellectuals had been traumatized; they would ever after see history in the light of the past, all crowds through their memories of the Third Reich.

Certainly, radical movements attract paranoid personalities. Their ruling passion is hate, and they will follow anyone who promises to destroy the things they hate. But Americans have little sympathy with these people. The majority of Americans will not blindly follow a leader, good or bad. Moreover, the States are large and various, and there are many avenues to power; it is impossible for any one group to find and seize a position from which all the avenues can be commanded.

The confusion of American democracy is its strength. Europeans have never been able to understand this. They receive every bad piece of news from the States, every item of violence, as though it were an omen of total catastrophe—and so, indeed, it would be, if the States were like Europe.

Europeans have never understood the open society, the struggle for freedom, and the belief in the ability of the common man ultimately to make the right decision. The confusion in an open society is greater, but the decision will be a better one for the people in general.

Americans believe in the common man. Europeans never have been able to.

What many Europeans dislike about America is that it reminds them of this. America reminds them of what it would be like to be free, without a ruling class. They resent being reminded and urged to struggle for their freedom. Over and over, they have been on the verge of giving up the struggle to be free. Europe is the Sibyl in a cage—when the boys asked her what she wanted she said, "I want to die." More than once America has dragged Europe back from dying. No wonder they resent America.

XLI

I went back to poetry-readings against the war. There was a reading at Berkeley and another at Longshoremen's Hall in San Francisco. Poets of different kinds would find themselves side by side on the platform. At Longshoremen's Hall I read with Robert Duncan and Allen Ginsberg. Ginsberg had just come from seeing the Hell's Angels; he had been persuading them not to attack the protest-marchers. A few days before, we had marched from Berkeley to Oakland and, just as we got to the Oakland line, the Hell's Angels drove their motor-cycles into the line of march and a few people were hurt. So Ginsberg had been talking to the Hell's Angels, and he actually persuaded them to lay off. He said they were "a sweet bunch of guys".

I went to a "read-in" at Reed College in Oregon. The students sat for hours listening to the poets, some of whom had come a thousand miles to read their poems and speak against the war. After that I went to several readings with the same purpose. The readings were effective when each participant was asked to read for only ten minutes—and read something relevant to the war. Otherwise the evening dragged on, with the first readers taking all the time and exhausting the audience.

Some of the speakers would use the opportunity to talk about anything that came into their heads. At a reading that was supposedly against the war in Vietnam, one man read a translation that went on for half an hour and had no relationship to the war; another read a long chapter of ordinary non-political poetry reading I would read two or three poems against the war and make a few remarks. Politics then seemed to be part of my thought as a whole. After all, I was protesting because I was a poet—because a country that accepted this war would not be a country in which I could write poems—I was not writing poems in order to protest. My remarks therefore struck the audience as natural and persuasive. If there were people in the audience who did not agree with my opinions—and unlike protest meetings, where everyone was of the same mind, at ordinary poetry readings there would be pro-administration people—they might be won over or at least shaken in their convictions. At any rate I was reading poems and at the same time expressing my politics, without distorting either. Politics without poetry must surely be destructive; and, in the present climate, a writer who wishes to leave out politics will have to leave out what he sees and hears every day.

XLII

Greg was "expanding his consciousness". He had been on several LSD trips and ran an art gallery where he carried on "multi-sensory" experiments. Sometimes he drove over from San Francisco and came to the cabin where I worked with the blinds drawn, a dim room with only a cone of electricity shining in the middle, and tried to persuade me to stop thinking and just let everything happen. Through

a terrible novel. At a reading in New York, midway through the evening, a man made a rambling speech in defence of pigeons; we thought he must surely be an *agent provocateur*. In Philadelphia a poet got up on the stage, pointed to the flag, and said, "Let's get that rag out of here." By such gestures some of the performers attempted to win a moment of recognition for themselves.

What good did the protest-readings do? As most of the audience was already persuaded, the readings made few converts. But they did give the participants a sense of community. Writers who had nothing else in common found that they had indignation at least. The war in Vietnam was our Dreyfus case, dividing the country in two, and all kinds of personal reservations and fine distinctions went by the board. I thought that I was beginning to understand what the Russians had meant by an "intelligentsia". The intelligentsia were a class, rather than people who shared a positive conviction. They were people who were forced together by circumstances, so that their own individual reservations about art and other matters seemed unimportant. The war in Vietnam was creating an American intelligentsia, people who had to stick together in order to survive, and this feeling would remain after the war had ended.

There were few good poems written in direct response to the war. Most occasional poetry is bad, and the Vietnam poems were made out of what the poet had seen on TV or read in the papers. There was lacking the personal connection between the man and the subject—the feeling that only this man could have written this poem and that he had to write it—that is essential in poetry of any kind. Some of the poems were hysterical; there was a great deal of sheer paranoia being expressed. What was most common was a repulsive attitude of superiority—the poet berating the government and other people for not having his own sense of ethics.

In general the poems were tedious, because the ideas and language were journalistic. The following lines are typical of the poems about Vietnam and typical of polemic writing at any time.

Wednesday: What must we do before you hear us?
We march, teach, write, sing our anger,
paint banners in our blood,
burn up cards that bid us to the slaughter,
and in the ultimate scream ignite our flesh.

What must we do?

Thursday: Again and once again
the master pulls the strings,
demands consensus, and the puppets dance.
I tremble for my country
that we must walk with downcast heads,
ashamed.

And what will history tell of us
who let such monstrous things go on?

On the other hand the following lines from a poem by Goran Sonnevi affect the reader, for the poet has been able to make a movement of the imagination, putting himself physically into the situation. Through sense–perception he has taken you over to the other side.

We saw a film strip taken with
the Viet-Cong; we could hear
the muffled fluttering
of helicopter propellers
from the ground, from the side being
shot.

To be effective, political poetry must represent the

thought of a political man. The poems of the Chilean poet Neruda are political because he has transformed himself into a man who sees everything—an onion, a glass of wine, a butterfly—from the viewpoint of the poor. Just as everything that Alexander Pope wrote reflected the attitudes of the ruling class in London in his time, so Neruda's poetry speaks for the dispossessed of South America, because he has lived with the people, seen them at work and drunk with them in the cafés. Political poetry is no easier to write than any other kind. It requires engagement, and this, contrary to what many people think, is not merely the engagement of the rational mind with a subject that is in everyone's thoughts; it is the engagement of the whole man, his way of life, his sensitivity, so that whatever happens enters his consciousness profoundly and stimulates a response of his entire being. A true political poem, like all true poetry, is an original creation.

Poems of this kind, however, are not likely to please th public. They won't please the Left any more than th Right. Revolutionaries who want a new establishment w not want these poems. A poem by Yevtushenko about dialogue between a hydro-electric dam and a pyramid . that can be understood! You don't have to guess which w win the argument. A poem like that has a practical purp and serves society. But a poem about a man beating woman? Is this cultured? A novel that depicts Rus people as liars and drunkards. . . . This is a libel against State, and the authors of such works must be either crim or insane.

*

I was no longer taking part in protest-readings, found another way of protesting which, at the same gave me some feeling of enjoyment. In the course

my window that peered through a screen of redwood trees I would see him arrive in his red Jaguar for another afternoon of trying to persuade me to enter the universe. I told him the last thing I wanted was to expand my consciousness; I had all the consciousness I could stand—the silence of those infinite spaces appalled me, etc.—but he thought I was just being square and he was labouring to convert me.

Greg's Jaguar, his art gallery, his love of good food, were perfectly natural for a young man in California, even a poet, but from the start they were obstacles to my taking anything he said seriously. Of course this was an unwarranted prejudice; I had never been able to realize that we were in a new age, an affluent society, when poverty was no longer necessary for artists, when the heroes of the young would be successful movie directors and advertising men, and revolutionaries would be supported by their parents. It was my problem if I could not conceive of an "Ode to a Nightingale" being composed by a man driving eighty miles an hour to a Chinese restaurant. But of course I missed the point entirely. Why write the ode at all?

"Writing, writing, writing," Greg said, and he picked up the sheet of paper on my desk—a few lines of type surrounded with revisions. It looked like a convocation of centipedes.

"Listen," he said, "I brought you a terrific article. After you read this you won't want to write any more."

The article was by Timothy Leary, and Greg didn't wait for me to read it, he gave me a running paraphrase of the contents.

"Everything is energy. Life is a flow of energy. Now, people are made up of cells and other packages that receive the flow. It's biochemical. In childhood, at certain moments, we are imprinted—see what Leary calls it, 'a biochemical freezing of external awareness to stimuli'. You see, we're taught in childhood to cope with the things that are happening around us—self-preservation—so that the genes will be transmitted to the next generation. But this imprinting cuts out all the free flow of energy and consciousness. We're zombies, man. But now we've got the drugs and we can erase the imprints. With LSD we can get back in touch directly with the energy source. This is what Leary calls ecstasy. It's what philosophers used to talk about—but it's better with LSD. Let me read you what he says: 'Breathing exercises, monastic withdrawal, prolonged meditation, mantras, mudras, mandalas can produce a state of quietude and serenity but only rarely do their adepts report a blinding illumination, a whirling inundation of sensation, the unity through multiplicity, which characterize the direct neurological confrontation with energy processes outside the imprint. Today, anyone can have this experience by ingesting a psychedelic drug. Temporary freedom from imprints is almost guaranteed.'"

In Leary's view, as explained by Greg, books were only imprinting, a language of dead symbols that excluded direct, total awareness. The poems I liked were just representations of the external world expressed in symbols I had been taught in childhood. But the new poet would express the world he perceived with all his senses, the experiential world. He would develop new forms of art. He would no longer simply represent the external, but communicate his inner experiences. Psychedelic drugs would provide the creative experience and, by means of technology, especially moving pictures, a man would be able to communicate this experience, and the communication would be art. "Microbiological film technicians and physics-lab technicians thus become the philologists of the new language . . ."

The new poet would be a movie director. But I had better let Leary explain it. Art that attempts to record the experience of pure symbol-free energy we shall call Tranart. Using the letters LFI—Learned Form Images—meaning "representations of perceptual forms which are learned and artifactual. Objects, things, organisms, events, bodies, chairs, flowers"—and the letters DPI—Direct Process Images—meaning "externalized representations of the flow of direct sensation—experience. They must be flowing, unstructured, unidentifiable. They are communications of the experience of direct energy"—it is possible to describe what Tranart will be like. First you must have a library of Direct Process Images and Learned Form Images.

An ever-increasing library of catalogued DPIs and LFIs is thus assembled. It is even possible to play an experimental Hessean bead game with infinite combinations of images. More important, it is possible to express any experience—either of a non-cultural energy or life process or a visionary creation.

A subject wishes to record a visionary and cultural sequence. This requires a visionary tranart—LFIs imposed on or woven into DPIs.

There comes a vision of undulating streams of bouncing spheres (not recognized as blood cells) which convert (as an LFI is imposed on the primary process) into uncoiling serpent-flow which changes to an insidious network of Chinese Communist soldiers which shifts into the pink florid, pulsating face of a leering oriental dictator which flickers into the portrait of one's feared stepmother, etc., etc. That's the vision sequence.

To express this the subject sorts through the DPI library until he locates a blood circulation DPI. This stored film loop is set running on one projector. Then the subject finds an LFI sequence of uncoiling serpents. They are green, so he imposes a red filter. The DPI projector starts running; after a minute the red filter serpent LFI projector is snapped on—out of focus. Gradually, the LFI strip is brought into focus and the vision slowly shifts from pure DPI–LFI vision. The LFI film-strip is then spliced to newsreel film of marching Chinese columns and then the picture of Chou En Lai. A still photo of stepmother is inserted in the slide projector with a veined red filter completely out of focus and slowly focused at the appropriate second.

The Tranartist then experiments with his material until he gets the flowing sequence he wants, LFIs fading in and out of focus—with the pulsing DPI stream always flowing in the background. He speeds up the sequence many times, then he adds sound. The pump, pump, pump of a heartbeat fades into the thud, thud of marching feet, to the shouted "You bad boy, you'll never amount to anything." The sound sequence is adjusted to the visual barrage and speeded up. That's one minute or thirty seconds of the Tranart representation of a psychedelic vision.

This, then, was the art of the future. In the beginning was the Word, but from now on words would be unnecessary and poets would sit at the feet of film technicians. It was the triumph of American technology. The training of artists and creative performers, in Leary's view, would become "a straightforward, mechanical process." As for writing—"It is a simple task to teach a child to write experientially like Joyce."

After such sessions, when Greg roared off in his Jaguar, I was sadly outmoded, gazing at the sheets of paper on my desk with their scrawled revisions—"the rational mind 'damages' the brain" (Leary). I felt like a South Pacific native who had been presented with a Bible by a missionary. Cultural shock. My tribal customs were being wiped out. And yet, suppose what Leary said were true, did I have to like it? You don't have to fall down and worship a new juju just because it appears. Suppose that the new art of lab-technicians, rug-manufacturers, players of the "Hessean bead-game", prevailed everywhere, I would still prefer my "imprinting". Let them call what they did art and poetry. They could have those words, and I and others like me would find other words to describe the process to which we were addicted. Hooked, as Leary would say.

I was too deeply imprinted to be able to appreciate Tranart. Besides, no matter how seriously I tried to take the solemnities of this generation, cheerfulness kept breaking in. Whenever anyone declares the one true way of any-thing, I have an irresistible desire to laugh. Mario Savio was right—don't trust anyone over thirty. For you can't sell them a bill of goods.

Listening to Greg, a voice of the psychedelic generation, I was reminded of Marlowe's *Doctor Faustus*. When Faust signed away his soul and got in exchange the power to do anything he wanted, to call up colours and shapes and have all sorts of tactile experiences, he could think of nothing better than to go to Rome and hit some priests over the head with a bladder. True—he also summoned up a vision of Helen of Troy. The stage direction says she appears, but it isn't the direction or the acting that convinces us, it is Marlowe's imagining of Helen, and this takes place in words.

> O, thou art fairer than the evening air
> clad in the beauty of a thousand stars;
> Brighter art thou than flaming Jupiter
> When he appear'd to hapless Semele;
> More lovely than the monarch of the sky
> In wanton Arethusa's azur'd arms;
> And none but thou shalt be my paramour!

It is possible that Leary and others like Leary have not experienced words—therefore they need to be provided with pictures and sounds. It is possible that Marshall McLuhan never learned to read. When I read McLuhan's description of what happens when you read—one idea following another in sequence—then I am sure he never learned to read. The truth is that when you read, instead of one thing following another, all sorts of ideas come into the mind at the same time, and they come much faster and by subtler ways than from looking at film and listening to sounds. When you get your ideas by listening and looking, when your sense-perceptions are being manipulated by a machine, they must work at the pace of the machine. Mechanical and chemical processes are limiting; it is the machine or drug that expands its consciousness—while the mind shrinks. Those who submit to drugs and machines are limiting their minds. Thinking, on the other hand, is an active function of the whole living organism and is unlimited. In fact, it is indefinable, for the moment we defined it we would have ceased to think.

*

The fool in his generation prophesies for the next, and there were San Franciscans who spoke for Youth—that is, the hippies and flower children. "Youth will make this one of the most popular films ever produced! Dylan expresses something very, very, very important about the New Youth. Our sons and daughters are beyond our command, and he offers us clues as to why." A large number of Californians were ready to check their brains—what there were of them—and take their direction from children. California had never had much history; more and more the state was filling up with Southern crackers and old people from Ohio—if it wasn't ignorance it was senility—so that here, indeed, youth set the pace.

Was youth as happy about this as middle-aged newspapermen said it was?

"Everyone's having a ball," Greg told me. "Here, have another helping of pressed duck."

We were sitting on the floor, being served by his girl friend, while overhead a lantern constructed of metal planes revolved so that the room was moving around in flashes of colour. In one corner stood the press and other machinery with which he printed pamphlets and advertisements. A flier announced an exhibition of

avant-garde posters, manifesti,
objects, lithographs, books,
photographs, happenings kits
periodicals, memorabilia and
ephemera from today's
growing edge of international
underground activity;

neo-dada, concretism,
spatialism, the mediocres,
letterism, fluxus,
de-coll/age, etc

The walls were covered with art-nouveau posters—letters that swirled and receded, faces that peered through the letters, big eyes, thin Beardsleyesque bodies with long hair, stars, figures of the zodiac—purple, yellow, chartreuse, blue. There were photographs of naked people fornicating. The floor was littered with illustrations from old magazines —drawings of farm machinery, surgical operations, old military uniforms—pieces of which Greg would cut out and use as border illustrations for the pamphlets, fliers, books of poetry and philosophy that he published.

It certainly looked like fun, and he had a point: my wanting to find a justification for such activities was irrelevant. For Greg and his friends, the thing was *to be* NOW.

The new generation had an amusing way of dispensing

with legalities. For instance, someone had suggested "a possibility for the new community in the Haight–Ashbury to test the power of love". The police were to be "equipped with the words and mystique of an ancient mantra still used in India to disperse crowds and multitudes". Then suppose a crowd were gathered in front of either Tracy's or the Psychedelic Shop, "ecstatic and unaware of ourselves as an obstruction to pedestrian traffic", and the police were called on the scene—then, if instead of approaching the group with surly preliminaries: "Break it up, c'mon, move along", the police moved upon the gathering "chanting the dispersal mantra", the crowd would recognize it as such and obey. "Think a moment of the effect such an episode would have upon all concerned." The police would receive the love and joyousness of the hippies. An appropriate mantra might be the Japanese word "ikimasho", which means "Let's go".

I agreed that it would be a novel spectacle, especially at the station house where the police chief would be teaching the fuzz to say "ikimasho".

*

The child whose parents gave him a chemistry set for Christmas ran away with the fairies. He came to San Francisco and lived with other children. The one feeling they all had in common was a dislike of parents—yet they depended on parents for their food and shelter. These feelings were irreconcilable—better not to think about it. But you can't just not think about one thing—you have not to think about anything at all. With drugs you were happy and didn't have to think.

Hippies and flower children were different from political activists. There was a clear division between young people who wanted to change the world and those who wanted

266

to live through drugs, looking at colours and drifting with sounds. At times the hippies and activists looked alike, when they gathered in a park or walked in a parade, but the activists wanted to change the world and the hippies wanted to be left alone.

One thing they shared was music—a hill-billy beat, rhythms of the Bible Belt played on electric guitars with the sound up full.

> Rock is a tribal phenomenon, immune to definition & other typographical operations, and constitutes what might be called a 20th century magic.
>
> Rock seems to have synthesized most of the intellectual & artistic movements of our time & culture, cross-fertilizing them & forcing them rapidly toward fruition and function.
>
> Rock is a vital agent in breaking down absolute & arbitrary distinctions.
>
> Any artistic activity not allied to rock is doomed to preciousness & sterility.

This was the gospel voice out of the hills, the pounding of the redneck preacher. Those who listened would be saved, and those who didn't would be sorry.

When they listened to rock they were moved. At other times they seemed to have no connection. The activists had their "thing"—Civil Rights, the war in Vietnam, a dozen other causes that would be there tomorrow. But the rest were, A. E.'s phrase, vanishing in a penumbra. There was no tension in these lives and therefore no drama. Monotonous. Boring! When the world is just what you want to perceive, there is no need to be involved with other people.

Yet they talked of love. Were there ever people who talked so much about it? I was reminded of the man who had been admiring athletes on a beach who were always bicycling up and down. With their red cheeks they looked the picture of health. Then he realized: these are not the ones who are in possession of health—they are in search of it. And so it was with the flower children; they were the ones who didn't have love.

Such were the followers of Leary and McLuhan—readers, if they read at all, of *The Prophet* and *Siddhartha*. Ideas that had struck my generation as dreadfully boring had something to say to these people. But was this true? Wasn't it possible they were just as bored but, as they had never read or thought about anything important, didn't know how bored they were?

Sometimes I didn't know if I was awake or asleep. I had no more human remembrance & forgot what things were. I sat for hours drawing. The hot water heater was all I heard clearly. In the next room human beings were conversing, & I could make out only whispering shards of what they said.

They believed in astrology. They were expanding into the cosmos. They were approaching the Aquarian Age. But it is impossible to describe the thoughts of those who were drifting at this far verge.

In *The Oracle*, one of the "underground" newspapers that were beginning to mushroom, they interviewed one another.

Q: Oh, you think there will be a persecution thing?

A: Oh, my goodness! This Reagan business is the beginning of it right now. People are not going to be given free education, even though the Russians give their people free education. And they'll go way ahead of us & get to the moon before we do, if we're not going to educate these people the way they do.

O God, O California! There was probably no place in the world that had better scenery, and there was no sadder place in the world either. Here were all the disconnected people—farmers from Iowa who had lived in mud and now wanted only to doze in the sunshine; young women from Brooklyn with warts, whose politics were purely revenge; the children of swimming-pools in La Jolla and tennis courts in Connecticut. At night across the Bay the lights of Fairyland twinkled and beckoned. Here came all the lost people, to the end of America where there is nowhere to go but out of your mind.

6

XLIII

Apollon Grigoryev writes: "It is easy to believe in theories—and I cannot, no matter how I try." These words could serve for me as well, and for others who go through life with a constant uneasiness, a sense of being tossed about, verging on an explanation and never quite reaching it—while other people seem to have so much certainty, seizing on politics, art or religion with both hands, making themselves a definite place in the world. For Grigoryev and myself and other "unnecessary men" the explanation is never quite right, the answer eludes us, until we give up the struggle in despair or discover that we are old. Besides, there is always the hope that the longer you put off deciding, the greater, the more inclusive and profound the answer will be when it comes—until it is too late. Some of these "unnecessary men" are fortunate; at the last moment they do cross over and join the ranks of the "saved". Proust comes to mind; he was at the mercy of impressions—gestures, anecdotes, odours, pieces of furniture; then he discovered a theory of time. But for the most part such people merely drift; they inhabit the penumbra; they vanish, leaving no trace on thought or history. Wouldn't it be better to have a place in the Paradise of Fools, among the true believers in wrong theories, than to have no place at all?

Like Grigoryev's, my head is full of seemingly significant scenes, gestures, faces, words spoken, that have no significance because they are not connected and serve no purpose. "Experience," said Johnson, "is a hard school, but fools will learn in no other." And what if you don't learn anything?

Moreover, it isn't just my own experiences that are

273

obsessive, that come to me day and night as though this time surely they have something to declare, and then like the others don't "turn out", drifting into chaos, but also the experiences of other people. My mother tells a story about something she saw as a child, and this torments me as though it happened to myself. One night in Russia she looked out a window and saw a man being taken away in chains. It was one of her relatives, an old man with white hair. He had quarrelled with a neighbour over a piece of property and the neighbour denounced him to the police for "subversive political activity". He was innocent, yet he was sent to Siberia and never returned. I can hear the shuffling feet and see the head and shoulders of the prisoner and his shadow cast on a wall. So I rush out to buy a copy of Chekhov's book on the penal colonies. At the present time, seventy years after the event, I am concerned with the administration of justice in Tsarist Russia. A fat lot of use that is!

Or I read a book about the Communist uprising in Paris in 1871. When the Communists surrendered they were roped together and marched, men, women and children, to the outskirts of the city. Too bad for the working-man who had the mark of a rifle-butt on his shoulder, or hands blackened with powder! The Government troops stopped a chimney-sweep, and his hands were black, so they shot him. They brought the prisoners in front of a table where General Galliffet was presiding, the hero of Sedan, and Galliffet said, "You have heard that I am merciless. Well, I am worse than you could imagine." Then the prisoners were taken out and shot. Don't Galliffet's words make your blood curdle? But what good is that?

It's not that I don't have ideas. For example, the matter of the Commune . . . if I were a professor, a real one, I'd work up a thesis explaining that the origins of the struggle between Communism and Capitalism in the twentieth century are not economic, as has been thought, but personal, a blood-feud, the kind of hatred that starts between families and goes on for its own sake, with incidents always being found to justify it. The rich and poor hate each other in their guts; it's a physical reason, based on the way people talk and blow their noses. When the Communists came to power in Russia they had all those people shot in order to wipe away the memory of Galliffet's smirk. So they perpetuated the blood-feud. I can see the thesis standing on a shelf: *Notes Toward a Study of the Psychological and Cultural Origins of the Capitalist–Communist Struggle.* I can even see the footnotes. And as I can see them, why should I write the thesis?

Having a belief is not so much a matter of being intelligent as of being hungry. Some people, whom Grigoryev calls *hommes forts*, have strong appetites for fame, money, women. In order to serve their appetites they seize life with both hands. They glut themselves, and to justify this they get up a theory, they say that they believe. The rest of us have weak appetites, and so we are always thinking "yes—but". For an excuse we say that we are intelligent. But the universe has enough intelligence. What the universe wants is something to happen, in any form whatsover, a little excitement—explosion of gases, liquefaction, solidification, formation of rocks, solid heads. From the viewpoint of the universe, thought is nothing and vacuity is terribly boring. From there even a dinosaur looks good and any theory is better than no theory at all.

Of course, artistic people think they are more than merely intelligent. Even a Grigoryev says, "I am greedy for life." Artistic people have to think so, for their vocation is providing nourishment for others, so they think that they themselves are capable of consuming and regurgitating masses of material. But in comparison with your real, full-grown meat-eaters they are only children. People with

275

artistic temperament, "sensitive" people, overrate their capacity. They don't have enough experience; they simply have no idea what goes on in the way of consumption in normal middle-class families.

People such as Grigoryev and myself who have no convictions are likely to be superstitious. *Déjà vu*—we think we have been here before. Prophecy—we have a vision of a strange room, and twenty years later we find ourselves inside it. Spilled salt, a ring around the moon, a line of poetry read by accident, strike us as having an ominous, personal application. We are always brooding over coincidences. Three times in the same day a man walks past carrying a ladder, and we think there is some significance in ladders. So we sit down to write a poem, "Ladders", and of course it doesn't work out. A practical man would think they are painting a house on the next corner. He might be mistaken, but at least he wouldn't cut himself shaving. Or we see pregnant women everywhere, and surely this is a manifestation of some great change in the world. We do not consider that there are always pregnant women. The difference is in our own psychological condition; on this day we happen to have, for personal reasons, an unusual interest in pregnancies.

Poets are particularly sensitive to things happening over and over again, and to juxtapositions of different things. These are rhythm and metaphor, and they comprise the better part of most poets' writings. It would be enough to write lines with rhythm and metaphor, but everyone else has a theory, so we must have one too, and then we write philosophy. The philosophy of poets is the despair of philosophers. The poet speaks of time and reality, but his explanation is only a means of justifying himself, of organizing and using the materials.

This is what happened to Proust. When his parents died he discovered that he, too, had a digestive system. He too was a weight-lifter, a strong man with an enormous appetite, incredible will-power. And this had been true from the beginning. He had even developed asthma in order to put people off and not be interrupted in his gathering of materials. Now that his parents were dead, he could let himself go. And now, if the reader will go back a few pages where I was talking about Proust, he will see what I mean when I say that I have no consistency, that like Grigoryev, "I can never contemplate an object from any single aspect". I cannot even think about Proust with any consistency for a few minutes. "My thinking is somehow kaleidoscopic. That's just the word!"

As I've said, we are troubled by coincidences. What, for example, am I to make of Ginsberg, who comes into my life again and again, and always at a crucial moment? Or is it his coming that makes the moment seem crucial? Our paths keep meeting and diverging. I meet him in New York when we are both young and "neurasthenic"—the doctor's very word. Then I am working in a publishing house and Ginsberg comes to see me because he is leaving for Mexico. We have nothing, really, to say to each other, we just stare. Yet his departure seems significant, as does my continuing to sit there reading bad manuscripts. Years pass and I hear that he has written a famous poem. I read it, and run to the typewriter to write a parody of it, and just as I'm licking the envelope there's a knock on the door. It's Ginsberg! At this moment of all moments! More years go by. I am living in Rome, and one day I decide to go and see the Sistine Chapel. I have never been here before, and here is Ginsberg coming toward me, from the middle of the Last Judgment. Years later, in California, I am asked to read poems protesting against the war in Vietnam, and I find myself side by side with Ginsberg on a platform. He now has a beard and a pot-belly, like Socrates. A few years more, and I see him sitting on the steps of a house at Port

Jefferson, ringing bells and chanting an Indian song to calm two men who are fighting on the lawn. Should I write an article about all this? Or a fictionalized version in the manner of Beerbohm? Nobody cares about such things nowadays, and besides, what would it prove? So instead of writing I go fishing.

> letting the line drift with the current,
> skirting the shadows of rocks . . .

Grigoryev and I are hoping to be convinced. We hope that one night when the moon has risen an angel will appear and say, "Take this down". According to Rilke this is what happened to him at Duino. An angel gave him the elegies. But with us it happens otherwise. The angel appears, dictates a few lines, looks at his watch, and vanishes. And there we are, with a handful of words. The worst of it is, these fragments don't vanish; they keep repeating themselves like a damaged record. They keep creeping into any new thing we are trying to write, where they don't belong, spoiling any new idea we may have. For example:

> I am swept in a taxi
> to the door of a friend.
> He greets me like a statue
> fixed in the position of a man
> who always marries the wrong woman.

These lines came to me three years ago, and have been returning ever since, and I can't exorcize them. They are the beginning of a poem about New York, the comedy of Chekhov brought over to verse, that will never be written.

But how can I tell? Maybe it will be written. For I've had other fragments that managed to come together, one day when I wasn't thinking about them too hard. Also, sometimes by sheer hard work I've managed to make sense out of such things. So just waiting isn't an answer—it's necessary to try. Yet, as I've said, there's no guarantee that if you keep trying anything will come of it.

Grigoryev and I keep looking out of the window when we should be listening to the lecture. I remember, when I was a schoolboy, three lines gouged in the desk along which you could run a pencil-point like a locomotive, switching from one line to another, but I don't remember how to use a slide-rule. I can remember the chapel floor under my knees but I don't remember the sermon. As for scenery—to people of our sort a landscape can be a disaster. Really you ought to keep your eyes closed to trees, mountains and so on, if you want to get ahead in the world. It may be that my whole life has been "conditioned" by the view from my window when I was a boy—curtains stirring, waves rushing toward me, coconuts thumping in the wind, seagulls. Even when I was asleep I could hear the sea.

Sense-perceptions are a hindrance to anyone who wants to make a career. Take literature, for example. Whenever by chance I come across *The New York Review of Books* I am amazed at the certainty those writers have, their ability to generalize, the clarity of their ideas, their lack of sense-perception. They are informed about everything—the latest news of politics, art, the theatre—and they go straight to the point. Reading those writers I understand how they can say that story-telling and poetry are dead and journalism is the only thing that matters. Grigoryev and I could never write like that. We are obsessed with a handful of words, the way a branch keeps tapping against the window. If history were left to people like us, what a botch we'd make of it! I was once involved in a revolution, and what I remember best is the bicycle I rode from place to place. I lived for a year in Italy, visiting the cathedrals, and what I remember most clearly is a patch of wall—earth-colour, with a poster, one corner of which had been torn off—on the *Via* Something or Other.

XLIV

"Poetry," Wallace Stevens said, "is a process of the personality of the poet." To have poetry we must have living men—and I might add that to have living men we must have poets, but this is a prejudiced view and I cannot prove it.

We talk about history and ideas, but it all depends on who turns up. We are like people in a besieged castle looking out on an empty world. We can calculate how to divide the food and water, but if no one comes up the road we are finished. So far someone has always come, and life and poetry are what he brings.

★

The Russian poet Andrei Voznesensky was visiting the States. The magazines carried articles about him and translations of his poems. His lecture agency called from New York to say that he wished to visit San Francisco, and they asked me to arrange a reading for him at Berkeley. A few days later he was delivered to a hotel room and I went to see him. I met a slender man of middle height with a round face and straight brown hair, the kind of Slavic baby face you see in Russian movies. He spoke very little English, just enough to enable me to understand the right order for the reading of his poems, which were in translations clipped out of magazines, and for him to express his wish not to discuss political matters with members of the press.

The reading was at eight. I went to pick him up at 7.30. On the way out of the hotel he said that he wanted two eggs. When I asked how these were to be cooked he said that he wanted them raw. I explained this to the woman sitting at the door of the hotel restaurant, adopting for the purpose a Hollywood version of Slavic: "I have here a Russian poet, and he wishes to eat two raw eggs. Could you give me two raw eggs, please."

As we were driving over to the reading Voznesensky said that he wanted some tea. I managed to get two cardboard containers of tea from a diner. It was nearly eight o'clock, and I was afraid that he would now ask for some *borscht*. But we got to the hall where the reading was to take place. It was packed. Before Voznesensky went on stage he cracked one of the raw eggs against the wall and swallowed it down, like some sort of woodland animal.

When we were on the stage—I was to read the translations aloud—the microphone didn't work. "Typical capitalistic technological inefficiency," someone remarked loudly in the front row. There was something about reading poetry in translation that turned everyone into actors performing in a B movie.

I read the translation of the first poem, "Goya", then Voznesensky read it in Russian. Out of the medium-sized body and child-like face came a loud, strong voice that shook the walls—waves of Russian, sounds that crashed about our ears. There was hardly any resemblance between the sounds coming out of Voznesensky and the words I had read in English. The audience was amazed, struck silent, and at the intermission there was a storm of applause. The reading lasted an hour and a half, ranging from dramatic poems to other poems in which humour predominated. At times his voice sank and he seemed to talking to an intimate friend. It was an operatic performance, and when it was over people came running up the aisles to shake his hand.

The next day someone told me that this was the first time he had understood what poetry was all about. He was a graduate student in English, and this comment reinforced an idea I had been having for some time—that poetry was not at all what it was said to be in graduate schools. There was an element in poetry that was not discussed in classrooms or in so-called critical papers—the effect of poetry when it is read aloud. As most American poems are written for the eye, and as most readings of poetry by Americans are feeble, the absence of this element is not noticed. But when a poet such as Voznesensky reads, the sound of the words and the construction of the poem as drama are overwhelmingly evident. There is a dramatic relationship between the poet and the audience, and the poem has an effect not unlike that of a piece of music. But what we have been calling criticism has no language in which to discuss these matters. These days, more and more poets are reading their poems aloud, and some are writing poems for this purpose. There is no shortage of poems, what is lacking is criticism. Contrary to what we have been saying for years, this is an age of poetry, and the critics are hopelessly out of touch. They have been learning to explicate words on the page while the poetry of the time has been taking place as a dramatic performance.

I walked around Berkeley with Voznesensky. He wanted to buy a shirt. I took him into a haberdashery where he made straight for a display of summer shirts and took one after another off the racks—shirts of synthetic materials in irridescent colours, shirts with patterns on them—coconut trees, naked footsoles, guitars, wild animals. Just the thing for Leningrad!

As we walked along the streets he talked about life in Russia. There, he said, poets were as important as congressmen, and when the poets spent an evening together reading their latest works, the next day everyone in Leningrad and Moscow knew about their new poems and what they had said about politics. I told him that things were very different in America; here nobody cared what poets thought about anything. Voznesensky's books were published in editions of a hundred thousand; an American poet could not expect to sell more than a thousand copies of his book.

He left to give a reading in San Francisco where he was taken up by the City Lights people; he went to a cabin in the country for a few days, and then flew back to New York. As it happened I was travelling that way myself, so we flew together. Voznesensky was exhausted and slept until we were over Salt Lake City. When he awoke he plunged into a story about an artificial lake in Russia that had been constructed to cover the graves of Jews killed in the war. He had been fishing in the lake and suddenly had the weird feeling that the fish were Jewish people. I talked to him, in return, about my Russian relatives. If my mother's family had not come to America I might have been in the lake myself. And if I had escaped I would probably have been talking to him about poetry just the same—somewhere in Russia instead of 30,000 feet above the Rockies. I don't know which to wonder at more: the way life drives people apart, disperses nations and wipes out records, or the way it brings toward each other, from different parts of the earth, people who have an interest in common.

I left him outside an apartment building in lower Manhattan. I was relieved that he was safe; after all, he was a sort of state treasure, and I had had a feeling that we were being followed by men in trench coats.

From time to time I receive a postcard from Andrei with no return address. I have read in the *Times* that he criticized the Writers' Union, the all-important organization of Russian writers that you have to belong to if you want to publish anything.

★

They come from every direction, poets from every country. Some of them are completely unknown to you, but it seems they are famous in their own language. They have been invited to the World Poetry Conference and have accepted eagerly.

There is the New York poet who is dressed in high Mod, with frills on his shirt. He keeps looking at himself in mirrors. If poetry were what fashionable people think it is, then this would be a great poet.

Nicanor Parra is here from Chile. On the first night of the conference he pleases the audience greatly; his *Antipoems*, humorous and iconoclastic, suit the taste of the audience, young people who want the personal voice of a man— informality, surrealism, insults to the Establishment.

> For half a century
> Poetry was the paradise
> Of the solemn fool.
> Until I came
> And built my roller coaster.
>
> Go up, if you feel like it.
> I'm not responsible if you come down
> With your mouth and nose bleeding.

The World Poetry Conference goes on for three days. On the second night the Polish poet Zbigniew Herbert reads his poems. This man is more serious. I feel that I understand him as I understood Voznesensky, and that if it had not been here on Long Island we would have met somewhere in any case and read our poems and talked to each other.

It is not a question of speaking about the same subjects or having the same opinions. It is a question of listening for the sense that things are making just a little beyond the words we already know.

284